AF615697

The Last Word on MAKING MONEY

The Last Word on MAKING MONEY

Compiled by Rolf B. White

Lyle Stuart Inc. *Secaucus, New Jersey*

Published by Lyle Stuart, Inc.
120 Enterprise Ave., Secaucus, N.J. 07094
In Canada: Musson Book Company
A division of General Publishing Co. Limited.
Don Mills, Ontario

Queries regarding rights and permissions should be addressed to: Lyle Stuart, 120 Enterprise Avenue, Secaucus, NJ 07094

Manufactured in the United States of America

ISBN 0-8184-0475-2 (Hardcover)
ISBN 0-8184-0480-9 (Paperback)

Preface

This book is a miscellany of quotations and quips, sayings and satire, wisecracks and witticisms, proverbs and precepts, dictums and doggerel, epigrams and aphorisms, truisms and adages, axioms and maxims, poems and rhymes, limericks and graffiti arranged as an anthology.

That's what it is, but forget it!

Treat it as an interesting Financial Digest and you have a unique collection of the best that has been said or written about making money from all over the world since records began. This can be used to improve your own performance and as a source of information to repeat in letters, speeches or everyday conversation. With this book you can impress others with your wit and wisdom and get the "last word" in *first.*

More than that, it is a fund of hints and useful tips, memory joggers and general guidance to assist you in making money, keeping it and then making more. If it fails sometimes to show you infallible methods of becoming rich, at least you can learn from the many examples of how not to do it.

This is a book for inspiration and amusement at odd moments. Keep it where you do most of your creative thinking: this might be at work, by your bedside or in the smallest room in the house, but perhaps we ought not to recommend in your car, where so many people get their brilliant ideas.

Every time you turn to it, we hope that you will find something humorous and that you will learn or be reminded of an idea for your own benefit. If this does not happen, we must assume that you are either perfect or a perfect fool. As you are reading this book, neither is likely!

As far as possible, entries have been confined to the experiences and results of successful people, as examples of methods that have already proved correct in practice.

Judging by the number of entries on each subject, it is surprising how this follows one's own opinion of the important factors leading to financial success. Great emphasis is placed on holding onto money once you have it and the fact that you will never really make it without this ability.

The principle of getting it any way you can seems almost acceptable and one may begin to doubt the classical method involving prudence, honesty and trust.

The most fundamental factor in any financial transaction is trust. Individuals value more than anything else their hard won image of reliability. You do not have any doubts, when handing over money at the store, that you will receive the goods; but contrast that with buying privately or dealing with an unknown vendor. Here there is always a period of uncertainty, with either ready cash or letters of credit and bank references, before goods are delivered. The same principles apply internally with companies, where most of the procedures have as much to do with eliminating temptation as they are connected with the smooth running of the business.

Like most things in life, some parts of this book are better than others. Old-fashioned quotations are in, because often the cleverest ideas were originally recorded back in the old days and these more literary inclusions tend to be near the end of each chapter. If you find the going a trifle heavy, you can skip these sections, but, although the language may be somewhat pedantic, their meaning still holds good today.

The difference between this work and most other books about money is that the editor does not agree with everything in it. In fact, there is violent disagreement with the sentiments expressed in many of the items. It is up to the reader to interpret his or her own view, remembering always that an opposite opinion can provoke the correct response.

One of the advantages that go with the compilation of an anthology like this, is that the blame for what is said rests squarely with the author of each entry and not with the editor. This applies in particular to the anti-feminism and the male/female ratio of the subject matter. Any objections can be countered with the indisputable fact that the vast majority of recorded sayings were expressed by men and that, until recently, "man" was a popular collective word for the human race as a whole. That's our excuse and we're sticking to it!

It has taken many years to accumulate these prime remarks about money and, before I decided to produce this collection in bookform, the source of quotations was not always recorded. The result is that a very small number can only be acknowledged as anonymous. My apologies to those who may be offended by non-recognition and to anyone whom I was unable to contact for permission to use their material. Omissions will be rectified in subsequent editions.

Finally, following the title of this book, I suppose that I ought to add my final comment, and here comes the bad news: to make money *last*, you have to make it *first*.

R. B. W.

Contents

III INCOME

IV FINANCE

V BACKGROUND

VI METHOD

VII RISK

VIII ATTITUDES

IX PRINCIPLES

X DANGERS

The Last Word on MAKING MONEY

I MONEY

Making Money

Use every dime
All of the time
With all your best endeavor,
To get enough
Of the lovely stuff,
That when you're broke is never.

The entire essence of America is the hope to first make money—then make money with money—then make lots of money with lots of money.
PAUL ERDMAN

The art is not so much in making money but in making enough and keeping it! ANON

The happiest time in any man's life is when he is in red-hot pursuit of a dollar with a reasonable prospect of overtaking it. JOSH BILLINGS

I never made any money until I took off my pants. SALLY RAND

One must choose, in life, between making money and spending it. There's no time to do both. EDOUARD BOURGET

I've always felt that if you could develop an answer to a need, this was the way to make money. Most people are more anxious to make money than they are to find a need. And without the need, you're working uphill. BILL LEAR

The darkest hour in any man's life is when he sits down to plan how to get money without earning it. HORACE GREELEY

The easiest way for our children to learn about money is for you not to have any. KATHERINE WHITEHORN

I believe the power to make money is a gift of God . . . to be developed and used to the best of our ability for the good of mankind. Having been endowed with the gift I possess, I believe it is my duty to make money and still more money and to use the money I make for the good of my fellow man according to the dictates of my conscience.
JOHN D. ROCKEFELLER

I went into the business for the money, and the art grew out of it. If people are disillusioned by that remark, I can't help it. It's the truth.
CHARLIE CHAPLIN

The best way to make money is to make money. COUNTERFEITERS' SAYING

If only God would give me a clear sign! Like making a large deposit in my name at a Swiss bank. WOODY ALLEN

If you want to make money, go where the money is.
JOSEPH P. KENNEDY

Making money is easy—knowing what to do with it becomes a problem.
RING LARDNER

My father was never particularly interested in making money. And neither am I. He always said that if you do the right thing, and build your bridges strong, it will come automatically. PHILIP K. WRIGLEY

To make money last
You have to make it first. ANON

Nobody works as hard for his money as the man who marries it.
FRANK McKINNEY HUBBARD

There is a kind of shrewdness many men have that enables them to get money. It is the shrewdness of the fox after the chicken. A low order of mentality often goes with it. SHERWOOD ANDERSON

To make money one must be really interested in money.
ALDOUS LEONARD HUXLEY

To make money, make quantity. HENRY FORD

A man can make more money with less effort in the movies than in any other profession. GEORGE SANDERS

When asked what they would be prepared to do for $1,000,000, more people said they would go to jail for a year than would take their clothes off in public. ANON

He made money, because he honestly loved it with innocent affection. He was true to it. The reason you have no money is because you don't love it for itself alone. Money won't ever surrender to such a flirt.
FINLEY PETER DUNNE

Money's all right, but you can waste a powerful lot of time making it.
ANON

In order to make money the first thing is to have no need of it.
LUDOVIC HALÉRY

Money will come when you are doing the right thing.
MICHAEL PHILIPS

I always go where the dough is. GYPSY ROSE LEE

Money is the seed of money, and the first guinea is sometimes more difficult to acquire than the second million.
JEAN-JACQUES ROUSSEAU

You want to know how I make my money? There are two million fools born for every intelligent man. ARNOLD ROTHSTEIN

To force myself to earn more money, I determined to spend more.
JAMES AGATE

A people so primitive that they did not know how to get money except by working for it. GEORGE ADE

I did it for the money. ALFRED KRUPP

Many an optimist has become rich simply by buying out a pessimist.
LAURENCE J. PETER

If making money is a slow process, losing it is quickly done.
IHARA SAIKUKU

There is something about making money. You can bitch at it and talk about your ego, but make money and it all becomes easy. It even improves your personality.
JOHN M. KING

There are two types of people: those who cannot make it, and those who cannot keep it.
EVAN ESAR

If a man has money, it is usually a sign, too, that he knows how to take care of it; don't imagine his money is easy to get simply because he has plenty of it.
EDGAR WATSON HOWE

Almost any man knows how to earn money, but not one in a million knows how to spend it.
HENRY DAVID THOREAU

It is worth a thousand pounds a year to have the habit of looking on the bright side of things.
SAMUEL JOHNSON

Make money, and the whole world will conspire to call you a gentleman.
MARK TWAIN

Be the business never so painful, you may have it done for money.
THOMAS FULLER

I cannot afford to waste my time making money.
JEAN LOUIS AGASSIZ

Making money is fun, but it's pointless if you don't use the power it brings.
JOHN BENTLEY

Much work is merely a way to make money; much leisure is merely a way to spend it.
C. WRIGHT MILLS

To learn the value of money, it is not necessary to know the nice things it can get for you, you have to have experienced the trouble of getting it.
PHILIPPE HERIAT

The first of all English games is making money.
JOHN RUSKIN

The money men make lives after them. SAMUEL BUTLER

Those who help us make money seldom lose all our esteem.
J. PETIT-SENN

Definitions of Money

I've always wondered why it's so,
That money never lingers.
Now I know why it's called "dough,"
It sticks to other's fingers.

Money is what you'd get on beautifully without if only other people weren't so crazy about it. MARGARET CASE HARRIMAN

Money is the god of our time, and Rothschild is his prophet.
HEINRICH HEINE

Money doesn't always bring happiness. People with ten million dollars are no happier than people with nine million dollars.
HOBART BROWN

Money is round. It rolls away. SHOLEM ALEICHEM

Money is more troublesome to watch than forget.
MICHEL de MONTAIGNE

If you can actually count your money, then you are not really a rich man.
PAUL GETTY

Money is the fruit of evil and often is the root of it. HENRY FIELDING

Money is the poor people's credit card. MARSHALL McLUHAN

What's money? It's the only thing that's handier than a credit card.
ANON

Money is a stupid measure of achievement, but unfortunately it is the only universal measure we have. CHARLES STEINMETZ

Money is paper blood. BOB HOPE

Money is an article which may be used as a universal passport to everywhere except Heaven, and as a universal provider of everything except happiness. *The Wall Street Journal*

Money is the only substance which can keep a cold world from nicknaming a citizen "Hey, you!" WILSON MIZNER

Money is so unlike every other article that I believe a man has neither a legal or a moral right to take all that he can get. PETER COOPER

Money has no ears, but it hears. JAPANESE PROVERB

Money is always there but the pockets change; it is not in the same pockets after a change, and that is all there is to say about money.
GERTRUDE STEIN

Money has little value to its possessor unless it also has value to others.
LELAND STANFORD

Money is a singular thing. It ranks with love as man's greatest source of joy. And with his death as his greatest source of anxiety.
JOHN KENNETH GALBRAITH

Money, which represents the prose of life and which is hardly spoken of in parlors without an apology, is, in its effects and laws, as beautiful as roses. RALPH WALDO EMERSON

Money is the wise man's religion EURIPIDES

Maybe money is unreal for most of us, easier to give away than things we want. LILLIAN HELLMAN

Character is money; and according as the man earns or spends the money, money in turn becomes character.
EDWARD BULWER-LYTTON

Money is the power of impotence. LEON SAMSON

Power of Money

Some say this and some say that
But when all is said and done,
Money makes the plutocrat
And keeps him number one.

The only people who claim that money is not important are people who have enough money so that they are relieved of the ugly burden of thinking about it. JOYCE CAROL OATES

Money, it turned out, was exactly like sex, you thought of nothing else if you didn't have it and thought of other things if you did.
JAMES A. BALWIN

The chief value of money lies in the fact that one lives in a world in which it is overestimated. HENRY LOUIS MENCKEN

Money isn't everything but it's a long way ahead of what comes next.
SIR EDWARD STOCKDALE

Money talks. The more money, the louder it talks.
ARNOLD ROTHSTEIN

When a man needs money, he needs money, and not a headache tablet or a prayer. WILLIAM FEATHER

If a man runs after money, he's money-mad; if he keeps it he's a capitalist; if he spends it, he's a playboy; if he doesn't get it, he's a ne'er-do-well; if he doesn't try to get it, he lacks ambition; if he gets it without working for it, he's a parasite and if he accumulates it after a lifetime of hard work, people call him a fool who never got anything out of life.
VIC OLIVER

Money is not an aphrodisiac: the desire it may kindle in the female eye is more for the cash than the carrier. MARYA MANNES

When I was young I used to think that money was the most important thing in life; now that I am old, I know it is. OSCAR WILDE

A billion here, a billion there—pretty soon you're talking about real money. SENATOR EVERETT DIRKSEN

There is no fortress so strong that money cannot take it. CICERO

No one would remember the Good Samaritan if he only had good intentions. He had money as well. MARGARET THATCHER

It isn't enough for you to love money—it's also necessary that money should love you. BARON ROTHSCHILD

Money differs from an automobile, a mistress or cancer in being equally important to those who have it and those who don't.
JOHN KENNETH GALBRAITH

We ought to change the legend on our money from "In God We Trust" to "Money We Trust." Because, as a nation we've got far more faith in money these days than we do in God. ARTHUR HOPPE

Life is short and so is money. BERTOLT BRECHT

Two men were walking along a crowded sidewalk in a down-town business area. Suddenly one exclaimed, "Listen to the lovely sound of that cricket." But the other could not hear. He asked his companion how he could detect the sound of a cricket amid the din of people and traffic. The first man, who was a zoologist, had trained himself to listen to the voice of nature. But he didn't explain. He simply took a coin out of his pocket and dropped it to the sidewalk, whereupon a dozen people began to look about them. "We hear," he said, "what we listen for."
KERMIT L. LONG

In national affairs a million is only a drop in the budget.
BURTON RASCOE

If American men are obsessed with money, American women are obsessed with weight. The men talk of gain, the women talk of loss, and I do not know which talk is the more boring. MARYA MANNES

Where money talks, there are few interruptions.
HERBERT V. PROCHNOW

Remember that time is money. BENJAMIN FRANKLIN

Time is money—says the vulgarest saw known to any age or people. Turn it round about and you get a precious truth—money is time.
GEORGE GISSING

I like Paris. They don't talk so much of money, but more of sex.
VERA STRAVINSKY

In an age when we would rather have money than health, and would rather have another man's money than our own, he lived and died unsordid. MARK TWAIN

When I had money everyone called me brother. POLISH PROVERB

It happens a little unluckily that the persons who have the most infinite contempt of money are the same that have the strongest appetite for the pleasures it procures. WILLIAM SHENSTONE

Money never goes to jail. ARAB PROVERB

It is extraordinary to what an expense of time and money people will go to get something for nothing. ROBERT LYND

I didn't inherit any money. MOE DALITZ

Money does not pay for anything, never has, never will. It is an economic axiom as old as the hills that goods and services can be paid for only with goods and services. ALBERT JAY NOCK

The man who damns money has obtained it dishonorably; the man who respects it has earned it. AYN RAND

A man's treatment of money is the most decisive test of his character—how he makes it and how he spends it. JAMES MOFFATT

I've realized, after fourteen months in this country, the value of money, whether it is clean or dirty. NGUYEN CAO KY

Money swore an oath that nobody who did not love it should ever have it.
IRISH PROVERB

It is a kind of spiritual snobbery that makes people think they can be happy without money. ALBERT CAMUS

In our culture we make heroes of the men who sit on top of a heap of money, and we pay attention not only to what they say in their field of competence, but to their wisdom on every other question in the world.
MAX LERNER

Trade is the mother of money. ANON

Jesus went into the temple and overthrew the tables of the money changers. *St. Mark*

What I as a human being cannot do, in other words, what all my individual faculties cannot do, I can do by means of MONEY. Hence money makes every one of these faculties into something which it is not in itself, i.e., turns it into its opposite. KARL MARX

We Americans worship the almighty dollar! Well, it is a worthier god than Hereditary Privilege. MARK TWAIN

Money does all things; for it gives and it takes away, it makes honest men and knaves, fools and philosophers; and so on to the end of the chapter. SIR ROGER L'ESTRANGE

The value of a dollar is social, as it is created by society.
RALPH WALDO EMERSON

Money is human happiness in the abstract; he, then, who is no longer capable of enjoying human happiness in the concrete devotes himself utterly to money. ARTHUR SCHOPENHAUER

It is true that money attracts; but much money repels.
CYNTHIA OZICK

Life and money—you can't separate them. Not on this planet. Not in the kind of life you have to live. THOMAS H. RADDALL

All things obeyen to moneye. GEOFFREY CHAUCER

Using Money

I really think it's rather funny
That people are so prone
To take more care of other's money
Than they do with their own.

Even it you can't take it with you, it can sure brighten up the port of embarkation. CY PEACE

We all know how the size of sums of money appears to vary in a remarkable way according as they are being paid in or paid out.
JULIAN SORRELL HUXLEY

Money is like an arm or leg; use it or lose it. HENRY FORD

Money is like manure. If you spread it around, it does a lot of good. But if you pile it up in one place, it stinks like hell.
CLINT MURCHISON, JR.

O money, money, money,
I'm not necessarily one
Of those who think thee holy,
But I often stop to wonder
How thou canst go out so fast
When thou cometh in so slowly. OGDEN NASH

Money doesn't buy happiness. It buys great hookers—but not happiness.
BURT REYNOLDS

Each of us has the choice—we must make money work for us, or we must work for money. CONRAD LESLIE

Money is like a sixth sense, and you can't make use of the other five without it. SOMERSET MAUGHAM

In investing money, the amount of interest you want should depend on whether you want to eat well or to sleep well. J. KENFIELD MORLEY

I was born into it and there was nothing I could do about it. It was there, like air or food, or any other element. The only question with wealth is what you do with it. JOHN D. ROCKEFELLER

Americans have an abiding belief in their ability to control reality by purely material means. Hence airline insurance replaces the fear of death with the comforting prospect of cash. CECIL BEATON

My boy, always try to rub up against money, for if you rub up against money long enough, some of it may rub off on you. DAMON RUNYAN

A liberal is a man who is willing to spend somebody else's money.
CARTER GLASS

Money brings only misery. But with money you can afford it.
GERALD F. LIEBERMAN

If a man is wise, he gets rich, and if he gets rich, he gets foolish, or his wife does. That's what keeps the money moving around.

FINLEY PETER DUNNE

The secret and the difference between winners and losers is in discipline. The winner manages his money. The loser lets the money manage him.

NICHOLAS DANDALOS

When you put your money to work for you, you'd better be prepared to work for it.

LEWIS OWEN

Give us the luxuries of life and we will dispense with necessaries.

OLIVER WENDELL HOLMES

The greatest humbug in the world is the idea that money can make a man happy. I never had any satisfaction with mine until I began to do good with it.

EARL of CAMDEN

I like to dive around in my money, like a porpoise and burrow through it like a gopher and toss it up and let it hit me on the head.

SCROOGE McDUCK

I can recall the moment when I shed poverty like an infected cloak. I had a speaking engagement and as usual dashed after a bus only to see it go off. I began to walk to save money and suddenly stopped short. I realized that I did not need to save twopence. I could afford half a crown for a taxi. I jumped into a taxi and arrived in style.

GEORGE BERNARD SHAW

He who draws upon his own resources easily comes to an end of his wealth.

WILLIAM HAZLITT

Never spend your money before you have it.

THOMAS JEFFERSON

Isn't it a shame that future generations can't be here to see all the wonderful things we're doing with their money?

HERBERT V. PROCHNOW

It is better to live rich than to die rich.

SAMUEL JOHNSON

Money is the most egalitarian force in society. It confers power on whoever holds it.

ROGER STARR

Money makes the mayor go.

OLIVER HERFORD

The American talks about money, because that is the symbol and measure he has at hand for success, intelligence and power, but as to money itself he makes, loses, spends, and gives it away with a very light heart.
GEORGE SANTAYANA

To have money is to have time. ALBERT CAMUS

Nine times out of ten money will do the trick required at the moment.
JOHN WAIN

Money, you know, will hide many faults. MIGUEL CERVANTES

When Gold argues the cause, eloquence is important.
PUBLILIUS SYRUS

Money is a handmaiden if thou knowest how to use it; a mistress if thou knowest not. HORACE

It is one thing to have a right to the possession of money, and another to have a right to use money as one pleases. POPE LEO XIII

The best way to attract money, she had discovered, was to give the appearance of having it. GAIL SHEEHY

If ever you have a lump of money large enough to be of any use, and can spare it, don't give it away: find some needed job that nobody is doing and get it done. GEORGE BERNARD SHAW

The good Lord gave me my money, and how could I withhold it from the University of Chicago? JOHN D. ROCKEFELLER

Get all you can, and what you can get hold: 'Tis the stone that will turn all your lead into gold. . . . Remember that money is of a prolific generating nature. Money can beget money, and its offspring can beget more. BENJAMIN FRANKLIN

Lack of Funds

If money does not do
As much for us as it did,
Perhaps we do not do
As much for it as we did.

Nothing is sadder than having worldly standards without worldly means.
VAN WYCK BROOKS

I can remember when you used to kiss your money good-bye. Now you don't even get a chance to blow in its ear. ROBERT ORBEN

Lack of money is the root of all evil. GEORGE BERNARD SHAW

To have money is to be virtuous, honest, beautiful and witty. And to be without it is to be ugly and boring and stupid and useless.
JEAN GIRADOUX

I owe much; I have nothing; the rest I leave to the poor.
FRANCOIS RABELAIS

When you're down and out something always turns up—and it's usually the noses of your friends. ORSON WELLES

When a man says money can do everything, that settles it; he hasn't any.
EDGAR WATSON HOWE

A deficit is what you have when you haven't got as much as you had when you had nothing. GERALD F. LIEBERMAN

I have the feeling that in a balanced life one should die penniless. The trick is dismantling. ART GARFUNKEL

There were times my pants were so thin I could sit on a dime and tell if it were heads or tails. SPENCER TRACEY

He who has no bread has no authority. TURKISH PROVERB

We haven't the money, so we've got to think. LORD RUTHERFORD

I've got all the money I'll ever need if I die by four o'clock.
HENNY YOUNGMAN

I would not say millionaires were mean. They simply have a healthy respect for money. I've noticed that people who don't respect money don't have any.
PAUL GETTY

I got what no millionaire's got, I got no money.
GERALD F. LIEBERMAN

Subject to a kind of disease, which at that time they called lack of money.
FRANCOIS RABELAIS

I must say I hate money but it's the lack of it I hate most.
KATHERINE MANSFIELD

Necessity knows no Sunday.
AGNES REPPLIER

The distance from nothing to a little is ten thousand times more than from it to the highest degree in this life.
JOHN DONNE

No one can worship God or love his neighbor on an empty stomach.
WOODROW WILSON

I know a fellow who's as broke as the Ten Commandments.
JOHN P. MARQUAND

If you have no money, be polite.
DANISH PROVERB

An optimist is always broke.
FRANK McKINNEY HUBBARD

Many of the optimists in the world don't own a hundred dollars, and because of their optimism never will.
EDGAR WATSON HOWE

Beggars can never be bankrupts.
AMERICAN PROVERB

Life is short and so is money.
BERTOLT BRECHT

A miser is ever in want.
GREEK PROVERB

They who have little are thought to have no right to anything.
JOHN LANCASTER SPALDING

A beggar's purse is bottomless. PROVERB

That I should make him that steals my coat a present of my cloak—what would become of business? KATHARINE LEE BATES

He is not poor that hath not much, but he that craves much. PROVERB

No man needs money so much as he who despises it.
JEAN PAUL RICHTER

He that wants money, means, and content, is without three good friends.
WILLIAM SHAKESPEARE

Pro Money

Take the "my" out of money
And you're left with a "one."
It's not much, my honey,
But it's better than none.

In America, it's the big nickel or nothing: in between, nothing but tundra. SAUL MALOFF

It frees you from doing things you dislike. Since I dislike doing nearly everything, money is handy. GROUCHO MARX

I'd like to be that man Paul that everybody's been robbing Peter to pay.
Chicago Tribune

The four secrets of happiness: money, money, money, money. ANON

Money speaks sense in a language all nations understand.
ALFRED BEHAN

Money talks, and it is the only conversation worth hearing when times are bad. FRED ALLEN

Money can't buy happiness but it can buy the kind of misery you prefer.
LAURENCE J. PETER

I do everything for a reason. Most of the time the reason is money.
SUZY PARKER

Sex is like money—very nice to have but vulgar to talk about.
TONIA BERG

Some people are more turned on by money than they are by love. . . . In one respect they're alike. They're both wonderful as long as they last.
ABIGAIL VAN BUREN

The populace may hiss at me, but when I go home and think of my money, I applaud myself.
HORACE

Money brings happiness all the while;
Send me some and watch me smile.
Money is money, my little sonny,
And a rich man's joke is always funny.
THOMAS E. BROWN

It doesn't matter if you're rich or poor—as long as you've got money.
JOE E. LEWIS

I don't like money actually, but it quiets my nerves.
JOE LOUIS

Money does not make you happy but it quiets the nerves.
SEAN O'CASEY

God lives in a box all week and comes out on Sunday in funny clothes to talk about money.
SEAN MICHAELS

Money is applause.
JACQUELINE SUSANN

Money is a guarantee that we may have what we want in the future. Though we need nothing at the moment, it insures the possibility of satisfying a new desire when it arises.
ARISTOTLE

Money is necessary—both to support a family and to advance causes one believes in.
CORETTA SCOTT KING

An idealist is a person who helps other people to be prosperous.
HENRY FORD

Help me to money and I'll help myself to friends.
THOMAS FULLER

My attitude is, "Don't give me an award, send me money."
LINDA RONSTADT

It's good to have money and the things money can buy. But it's good too, to check once in a while and make sure you haven't lost the things that money can't buy. G. H. LORIMER

Though confidence is very fine,
And makes the future sunny,
I want no confidence for mine,
I'd rather have the money.
ANON

Money talks. PROVERB

The atmosphere reeked of the delicious odor of unearned money.
PETER BLACK

Money is indeed the most important thing in the world; and all sound and successful personal and national morality should have this fact for its basis. GEORGE BERNARD SHAW

When it is a question of money, everybody is of the same religion.
VOLTAIRE

Money should circulate like rainwater. THORNTON WILDER

With money you are a dragon; with no money, a worm.
CHINESE PROVERB

A wise man should have money in his head, not in his heart.
JONATHAN SWIFT

I love money; just to be in the room with a millionaire makes me less forlorn. LOGAN PEARSALL SMITH

Money dignifies what is frivolous if unpaid for. VIRGINIA WOOLF

Money alone sets all the world in motion. PUBLILIUS SYRUS

Remember that money is of a prolific, generating nature. Money can beget money, and its offspring can beget more, and so on. Five shillings turned is six: turned again it is seven; and so on till it becomes a hundred pounds. The more there is of it, the more it produces at every turning, so that the profits rise quicker and quicker. He that murders a crown, destroys all that it might have produced, even scores of pounds.

BENJAMIN FRANKLIN

Some nations are said to have too much gold. Still, if you have to be afflicted with something, we don't know but that we would like gold as well as anything.

ANON

A feast is made for laughter, and wine maketh merry: but money answereth all things.

Ecclesiastes

Anti Money

It would be libel
To state that the Bible
Says that money is the root of all evil.
So get it off pat,
What it does say is that
LOVE of money is the root of all evil.

Money often costs too much.

RALPH WALDO EMERSON

Money doesn't go as far as it used to, but at least it goes faster.

GERALD F. LIEBERMAN

Anyone who tries to understand the money question goes crazy.

FRANK VALDERLIP

That money talks I'll not deny.
I heard it once: it said "Good Bye."

ANON

If you're problem's one real beaut,
Money's surely at the root.

Money brings some happiness. But, after a certain point, it just brings more money.

NEIL SIMON

I am not interested in money but in the things of which money is merely a symbol.

HENRY FORD

Why doesn't someone write a poem on money? Nobody does anything but abuse it. There's hardly a good word for money to be found in literature. The poets and writers have been needy devils and thought to brave out their beggary by pretending to despise it. This shows what liars poets and literary men are.

The chief cry of their hearts has never found its way into their books during the last 3,000 years. JOHN JAY CHAPMAN

Most men's hearts is located rather closer to their britches pocket than they are to their breast pockets. EDWARD NOYES WESTCOTT

As a general rule, nobody has money who ought to have it.
BENJAMIN DISRAELI

Money only appeals to selfishness and irrestibly invites abuse. Can anyone imagine Moses, Jesus, or Gandhi armed with the money bags of Carnegie? ALBERT EINSTEIN

Where there is money, there is fighting. MARIAN ANDERSON

A moderate addiction to money may not always be hurtful, but when taken in excess it is nearly always bad for the health.
CLARENCE DAY

It is my opinion that a man's soul may be buried and perish under a dung-heap, or in a furrow of the field, just as well under a pile of money.
NATHANIEL HAWTHORNE

Money never made a man happy yet, nor will it. There is nothing in its nature to produce happiness. The more a man has, the more he wants. Instead of its filling a vacuum, it makes one. If it satisfies one want, it doubles and trebles that want another way. That was a true proverb of the wise man, rely upon it: "Better is little with the fear of the Lord, than great treasure, and trouble therewith." BENJAMIN FRANKLIN

When money speaks, the truth keeps silent. RUSSIAN PROVERB

One of the evils of money is that it tempts us to look at it rather than at the things that it buys. EDWARD MORGAN FORSTER

Money doesn't do me any good. I can't spend it on myself. Money has no value, anyway. It is merely a transmitter, like electricity.
HENRY FORD

The gods are those who either have money or do not want it.
L. BUTLER

Money destroys human roots wherever it is able to penetrate, by turning desire for gain into the sole motive. It easily manages to outweigh all other motives, because the effort it demands of the mind is so very much less. Nothing is so clear and so simple as a row of figures.
SIMONE WEIL

In the race for money some men may come first, but man cometh last.
MARYA MANNES

The society of money and exploitation has never been charged, so far as I know, with assuring the triumph of freedom and justice!
ALBERT CAMUS

Money. A blessing that is of no advantage to us excepting when we part with it.
AMBROSE BIERCE

Make money your god, it will plague you like the devil.
HENRY FIELDING

Gold in families debate;
Gold does friendship separate;
Gold does civil war create.
ABRAHAM COWLEY

II WEALTH

Getting Rich

The right amount
Is paramount;
It will carry you.
There is one flaw,
If you get more;
You must carry it.

I'm opposed to millionaires, but it would be dangerous to offer me the position. MARK TWAIN

Someday my boat will come in—and with my luck I'll be at the airport. GRAFFITO

I'd give a thousand dollars right now to be a millionaire. HAL WILTON

Thou canst not serve God, unless thy mammon serve thee. ANON

How do you make a million?
You start with $900,000. STEPHEN LEWIS

Some men's domestic troubles drive them to drink, others to labor. You read about a man becoming a millionaire and think he done it by his own exertions when it was the fear of coming home empty-handed and dislike of staying around the house all day that made him rich.
FINLEY PETER DUNNE

It is hard to be poor when there are so many rich fools at whose expense one could live.
DENIS DIDEROT

A rich man and an ashtray—the more they collect, the dirtier they get.
JAPANESE PROVERB

Be kind to people until you make your first million. After that people will be nice to you.
ANON

The trick is to make sure you don't die waiting for prosperity to come.
LEE IACOCCA

A statistician says a man stands sixteen chances to be killed by lightning to one of being worth a million of money.
ANON

I do not believe in leaving children a great many millions of dollars.
HENRY FRICK

He who wishes to be rich in a day will be hanged in a year.
LEONARD da VINCI

If you want to get rich, you son of a bitch,
I'll tell you what to do:
Never sit down with a tear and a frown,
And paddle your own canoe.
ANON

I was lucky. When God rained manna from heaven, I had a spoon.
PETER F. DRUCKER

Working at it is better than wishing for it!
ANON

It ain't so much trouble to get rich as it is to tell when we have got rich.
JOSH BILLINGS

It takes a kind of genius to make a fortune, and especially a large fortune. It is neither goodness, nor wit, nor talent, nor strength, nor delicacy. I don't know precisely what it is: I am waiting for someone to tell me.
JEAN de la BRUYÈRE

Some people's money is merited and other people's is inherited.
OGDEN NASH

Barring some piece of luck I have seen but few men get rich rapidly except by means that would make them writhe to have known in public.
CHARLES DUDLEY WARNER

The rich only give to the rich. HELEN LAWRENSON

No man is rich whose expenditures exceed his means; and no one is poor whose incomings exceed his outgoings. THOMAS HALIBURTON

I think that the reason why we Americans seem to be so addicted to trying to get rich suddenly is merely because the opportunity to make promising efforts in that direction has offered itself to us with a frequency out of all proportion to the European experience. MARK TWAIN

The shortest and best way to make your fortune is to let people see clearly that it is in their interests to promote yours.
JEAN de la BRUYÈRE

It requires a strong constitution to withstand repeated attacks of prosperity. J. L. BASFORD

Where Vanderbilt sits, there is the head of the table. I teach my son to be rich. WILLIAM H. VANDERBILT

To suppose, as we all suppose, that we could be rich and not behave as the rich behave, is like supposing that we could drink all day and stay sober. LOGAN PEARSALL SMITH

To make a fortune some assistance from fate is essential. Ability alone is insufficient. IHARA SAIKYKY

There are two things needed in these days; first, for rich men to find out how poor men live; and second, for poor men to know how rich men work. EDWARD ATKINSON

I have no complex about wealth. I have worked hard for my money, producing things people need. I believe that the able industrial leader who creates wealth and employment is more worthy of historical notice than politicians or soldiers. PAUL GETTY

A man is rich in proportion to the things he can afford to let alone.
HENRY DAVID THOREAU

Be not concerned if thou findest thyself in possession of unexpected wealth; Allah will provide an unexpected use for it.
JAMES JEFFREY ROCHE

People who are hard, grasping . . . and always ready to take advantage of their neighbors, become very rich. GEORGE BERNARD SHAW

Wishing does not make a poor man rich. ARAB PROVERB

Riches amassed in haste will diminish, but those collected by little and little will multiply. JOHANN WOLFGANG von GOETHE

Most people believe that because a man has made a fortune his views on any subject are valuable. I have always believed that most large fortunes are made by men of ordinary ability who tumbled into a lucky opportunity and could not help getting rich, and in most cases, others given the same chance, would have done far better with it. Hard work and attention to business are necessary, but they rarely result in achieving a large fortune. Do not be fooled into believing that because a man is rich he is necessarily smart. There is ample proof to the contrary.
JULIUS ROSENWALD

He that maketh haste to be rich shall not be innocent. PROVERBS

Riches both make men happy while they are acquiring them, and give them a more pleasant life when they have acquired them.
GREEK PROVERB

Those who obtain riches by labor, care, and watching, know their value. Those who impart them to sustain and extend knowledge, virtue, and religion, know their use. Those who lose them by accident or fraud know their vanity. And those who experience the difficulties and dangers of preserving them know their perplexities. CHARLES SIMMONS

It is far more easy to acquire a fortune like a knave than to expend it like a gentleman. CHARLES CALEB COLTON

The pulpit and the press have many commonplaces denouncing the thirst for wealth; but if men should take these moralists at their word, and leave off aiming to be rich, the moralists would rush to rekindle, at all hazards, this love of power in the people lest civilization should be undone. RALPH WALDO EMERSON

The way to wealth is as plain as the way to market. It depends chiefly on two words, industry and frugality; that is, waste neither time nor money, but make the best use of both. Without industry and frugality, nothing will do; and with them, everything. BENJAMIN FRANKLIN

He is not fit for riches who is afraid to use them. ANON

Great pioneers like Huntington and Hill, men of daring and constructive genius like Harriman . . . did mighty work. True, they reaped rich rewards, but the wealth they received was but a trifling fraction of the wealth their work created for the people. OTTO H. KAHN

The production of wealth is not the work of any one man, and the acquisition of great fortunes is not possible without the cooperation of multitudes of men. PETER COOPER

It requires a great deal of boldness and a great deal of caution to make a great fortune; and when you have got it, it requires ten times as much wit to keep it. MEYER A. ROTHSCHILD

Freedom consists of the unimpeded right to get rich, to use this ability, no matter what the cost to others, to win advancement.
NORMAN THOMAS

Get Place and Wealth, if possible with grace;
If not, by means get Wealth and Place. ALEXANDER POPE

Wealth

We can say one thing for certain
About the affluent;
When they take that final curtain
They need not take a cent.

Wealth is the product of man's capacity to think. AYN RAND

Riches are the savings of many in the hands of one. EUGENE DEBS

If all the rich people in the world divided up their money amongst themselves, there wouldn't be enough to go round. CHRISTINA STEED

Just pretending to be rich keeps some people poor. ANON

True, you can't take it with you, but then that's not the place where it comes in so handy. BRENDAN FRANCIS

The average man is rich enough when he has a little more than he has got and not till then. WILLIAM RALPH INGE

If you aren't rich, you should always look useful.
LOUIS-FERDINAND CELINE

Wealth—Any income that is at least one hundred dollars more a year than the income of one's wife's sister's husband.
HENRY LOUIS MENCKEN

God help the rich, the poor can look after themselves.
ENGLISH PROVERB

If you want to know what the Lord God thinks of money, you have only to look at those to whom he gives it. MAURICE BARING

There are reckoned to be three times as many women than men who are worth more than $1 million ANON

I've been rich, and I've been poor; rich is better. SOPHIE TUCKER

People who have what they want are fond of telling people who haven't what they want that they don't really want it. OGDEN NASH

A man who has a million dollars is as well off as if he were rich.
JOHN JACOB ASTOR

It is no longer a distinction to be rich. . . . People do not care for money as they once did. . . . What we accumulate by way of useless surplus does us no honor. HENRY FORD

Until the age of twelve I sincerely believed that everybody had a house on Fifth Avenue, a villa in Newport and a steam-driven, ocean-going yacht. CORNELIUS VANDERBILT, JR.

Well, yes. You could say we have independent means.
JOHN D. ROCKEFELLER

You are affluent when you buy what you want, do what you wish, and don't give a thought to what it costs. J. P. MORGAN

Rich men without convictions are more dangerous in modern society than poor women without chastity. GEORGE BERNARD SHAW

Riches exclude only one inconvenience, and that is poverty.
SAMUEL JOHNSON

Be rich to yourself and poor to your friends. JUVENAL

If your riches are yours, why don't you take them with you to t'other world? BENJAMIN FRANKLIN

The time will never come when everybody is richer than everybody else.
C. E. AYRES

There'll be no pockets in your shroud. JAMES J. HILL

Wealth consists not in having great possessions, but in having few wants. EPICURUS

I don't think one can spend oneself rich. RHODA THOMAS TRIPP

I am absolutely convinced that no wealth in the world can help humanity forward, even in the hands of the most devoted worker in this cause.
ALBERT EINSTEIN

The rich would have to eat money, but luckily the poor provide food.
RUSSIAN PROVERB

How easy it is for a man to die rich if he will but be contented to live miserable. HENRY FIELDING

Some folks seem to get the idea that they're worth a lot of money just because they have it. SETH PARKER

The foolish sayings of a rich man pass for wise ones.
SPANISH PROVERB

Every man is rich or poor according to the degree in which he can afford to enjoy the necessaries, conveniences, and amusements of human life.
ADAM SMITH

He is a great simpleton who imagines that the chief power of wealth is to supply wants. In ninety-nine cases out of a hundred it creates more wants than it supplies.
ANON

The pride of dying rich raises the loudest laugh in hell. JOHN FOSTER

The concentration of wealth is made inevitable by the natural inequality of men.
WILL DURANT

A full cup must be carried steadily. ENGLISH PROVERB

Whoever is rich is my brother. RUSSIAN PROVERB

There are men who gain from their wealth only the fear of losing it.
ANTOINE RIVAROLI

Few of us can stand prosperity. Another man's, I mean.
MARK TWAIN

Prosperity is only an instrument to be used, not a deity to be worshiped.
CALVIN COOLIDGE

Riches serve a man, but command a fool. ENGLISH PROVERB

No man can tell whether he is rich or poor by turning to his ledger—It is the heart that makes a man rich—He is rich, according to what he is, not according to what he has.
HENRY WARD BEECHER

Wealth is the sinews of affairs. BION

The ass loaded with gold still eats thistles. GERMAN PROVERB

This, then, is held to be the duty of the man of wealth: First, to set an example of modest, unostentatious living, shunning display or extravagance; to provide moderately for the legitimate wants of those dependent upon him; and after doing so consider all surplus revenues which come to him simply as trust funds, which he is called upon to administer, and strictly bound as a matter of duty to administer in the manner which, to his judgment, is best calculated to produce the most beneficial results for the community—the man of wealth thus becoming the mere agent and trustee for his poorer brethren, bringing to their service his superior wisdom, experience, and ability to administer, doing for them better than they would or could for themselves. ANDREW CARNEGIE

Believe not much them that seem to despise riches, for they despise them that despair of them. FRANCIS BACON

Wealth, after all, is a relative thing, since he that has little, and wants less, is richer than he that has much, and wants more.
CHARLES CALEB COLTON

So long as a man enjoys prosperity, he cares whether or not he is beloved. MARCUS LUCAN

Benefits of Wealth

By those who ain't got it
Wealth is often abused.
But given a lot it
Is so rarely refused.

Wealth is not without its advantages and the case to the contrary, although it has often been made, has never proved widely persuasive.
JOHN KENNETH GALBRAITH

Money doesn't buy friends but it allows a better class of enemies.
LORD MANCROFT

A rich man is one who isn't afraid to ask the salesman to show him something cheaper. *Ladies' Home Journal*

The majority would prefer to be miserably rich than happily poor.
ANON

With money in your pocket, you are wise, and you are handsome, and you sing well too. JEWISH PROVERB

I'm so happy to be rich, I'm willing to take all the consequences.
HOWARD ABRAMSON

A man who has money may be anxious, depressed, frustrated and unhappy, but one thing he's not—and that's broke. BRENDAN FRANCIS

The life of the rich is one long Sunday. GEORG BÜCHNER

I'd like to be rich enough so I could throw soap away after the letters are worn off. ANDY ROONEY

All heiresses are beautiful. JOHN DRYDEN

The greatest luxury of riches is that they enable you to escape so much good advice. The rich are always advising the poor, but the poor seldom venture to return the compliment. SIR ARTHUR PHELPS

It must be great to be rich and let the other fellow keep up appearances.
FRANK McKINNEY HUBBARD

He has so much money that he could afford to look poor.
EDGAR WALLACE

He that is rich will not be called a fool. SPANISH PROVERB

In wealth many friends, in poverty not even relations. ANON

The rich man is everywhere expected and at home. SA'DI

Not even a collapsing world looks dark to a man who is about to make his fortune. ELWYN BROOKS WHITE

I have tried to teach people that there are three kicks in every dollar: one, when you make it—and how I love to make a dollar; two, when you have it—and I have the Yankee lust for saving. The third kick is when you give it away—and it is the biggest kick of all.
WILLIAM ALLEN WHITE

I'd like to live like a poor man with lots of money. PABLO PICASSO

Wealth is not his that has it, but his that enjoys it.
BENJAMIN FRANKLIN

Riches attract the attention, consideration and congratulations of mankind. JOHN ADAMS

Riches are not an end of life, but an instrument of life. HENRY WARD BEECHER

If a man who is born to a fortune cannot make himself easier and freer than those who are not, he gains nothing. JAMES BOSWELL

A man's true wealth is the good he does in this world. MOHAMMED

In big houses in which things are done properly, there is always the religious element. The diurnal cycle is observed with more feeling when there are servants to do the work. ELIZABETH BOWEN

The greatest and most amiable privilege which the rich enjoy over the poor is that which they exercise the least—the privilege of making them happy. CHARLES CALEB COLTON

Only the brave deserve the fair, but only the rich, fat, cowardly merchants can afford same. CHINESE PROVERB

Don't try to die rich but live rich. THOMAS BIRD MOSHER

I wish to become rich so that I can instruct the people and glorify honest poverty a little, like those kindhearted, fat, benevolent people do. MARK TWAIN

Wealth does not corrupt nor does it ennoble. But wealth does govern the minds of privileged children, gives them a particular kind of identity they never lose, whether they grow up to be stockbrokers or communards, and whether they lead healthy or unstable lives. ROBERT COLES

The privilege of the great is to see catastrophes from a terrace. JEAN GIRADOUX

It is extraordinary how many emotional storms one may weather in safety if one is ballasted with ever so little gold. WILLIAM McFEE

The world is his who has money to go over it. RALPH WALDO EMERSON

To be poor without murmuring is difficult. To be rich without being proud is easy. CONFUCIUS

The best way to realize the pleasure of feeling rich is to live in a smaller house than your means would entitle you to have. EDWARD CLARKE

Being very rich, as far as I am concerned, is having a margin. The margin is being able to give. MAY SARTON

The gratification of wealth is not found in mere possession or in lavish expenditure, but in its wise application. MIGUEL de CERVANTES

Nowadays, we think of a philanthropist as someone who donates big sums of money, yet the word is derived from two Greek words, philos (loving) and anthropos (man); loving man. All of us are capable of being philanthropists. We can give of ourselves. EDWARD LINDSEY

Gold will buy the highest honours and gold will purchase love. OVID

Disadvantages of Wealth

However much the whole world bitches
All about money's attendant hitches,
Called to account
Most would discount
The problems that accompany riches.

No Rockefeller in the record is ever known to have had a good time. LUCIUS BEEBE

It is tragic that Howard Hughes had to die to prove that he was alive. WALTER KANE

When the rich wage war, it's the poor who die. JEAN-PAUL SARTRE

It's possible to own too much. A man with one watch knows what time it is; a man with two watches is never quite sure. LEE SEGALL

Another bad thing about "prosperity" is that you can't jingle any money without being under suspicion. KIN HUBBARD

The prosperous man is never sure that he is loved for himself. MARCUS LUCAN

If you pick up a starving dog and make him prosperous, he will not bite you. This is the principal difference between a dog and a man. MARK TWAIN

You can't take it with you. MOSS HART and GEORGE KAUFMAN

Rich men feel misfortunes that fly over poor men's heads. ANON

One of the penalties of wealth is that the older you grow, the more people there are in the world who would rather have you dead than alive. C. H. B. KITCHIN

Since I am known as a "rich" person, I feel I have to tip at least $5 each time I check my coat. On top of that, I would have to wear a very expensive coat, and it would have to be insured. Added up, without a topcoat I save over $20,000 a year. ARISTOTLE ONASSIS

The more money an American accumulates, the less interesting he becomes. GORE VIDAL

Sometimes the pilgrimage from rags to riches is a journey from rate to wretchedness. R. W. HUBER

Poor men seek meat for their stomach, rich men stomach for their meat. ENGLISH PROVERB

The rich never feel so good as when they are speaking of their possessions as responsibilities. ROBERT LYND

Money alone can't bring you happiness, but money alone has not brought me unhappiness. I won't say my previous husbands thought only of my money, but it had a certain fascination for them. BARBARA HUTTON

For many men, the acquisition of wealth does not end their troubles, it only changes them. LUCIUS ANNAEUS SENECA

The rich are the real outcasts of society, and special missions should be organized for them. NORMAN MACLEOD

He who multiplies riches multiplies cares. BENJAMIN FRANKLIN

Keep company with the very rich and you'll end up picking up the check. STANLEY WALKER

We see how much a man has, and therefore we envy him; did we see how little he enjoys, we should rather pity him. JEREMIAH SEED

An accession of wealth is a dangerous predicament for a man. At first he is stunned if the accession be sudden, and is very humble and very grateful. Then he begins to speak a little louder, people think him more sensible and soon he thinks himself so RICHARD CECIL

Worldly riches are like nuts; many clothes are torn in getting them, many a tooth broke in cracking them, but never a belly filled with eating them. RALPH VENNING

Watch lest prosperity destroy generosity. HENRY WARD BEECHER

Let us not envy some men their accumulated riches; their burden would be too heavy for us; we could not sacrifice, as they do, health, quiet, honor and conscience, to obtain them: it is to pay so dear for them that the bargain is a loss. JEAN de La BRUYÈRE

To teach rich men to enjoy life would mean to ask them to give money away, which is difficult, to say the least. LI LIWENG

Better go to heaven in rags than to hell in embroidery. PROVERB

The rich man and his daughter are soon parted.
FRANK McKINNEY HUBBARD

A fortune is usually the greatest of misfortunes to children. It takes the muscles out of the limbs, the brain out of the head, and virtue out of the heart. HENRY WARD BEECHER

If you are poor, though you dwell in the busy market place, no one will inquire about you: if you are rich, though you dwell in the heart of the mountains, you will have distant relatives. CHINESE PROVERB

I have a rich neighbor that is always so busy that he has no leisure to laugh; the whole business of his life is to get money, more money, that he may still get more. He considers not that it is not in the power of riches to make a man happy; for it was wisely said that "there be as many miseries beyond riches as on this side of them." IZAAK WALTON

When you ascend the hill of prosperity, may you not meet a friend.
MARK TWAIN

For one rich man that is content there are a hundred that are not.
ANON

It is poor encouragement to toil through life to amass a fortune to ruin your children. In nine cases out of ten, a large fortune is the greatest curse which could be bequeathed to the young and inexperienced.
JEAN de la BRUYÈRE

Riches do not delight us so much with their possession as torment us with their loss. SAMUEL GREGORY

To acquire wealth is difficult, to preserve it more difficult, but to spend it wisely most difficult of all. EDWARD PARSONS DAY

The man who dies leaving behind him millions of available wealth, which was his to administer during his life, will pass away "unwept, unhonored and unsung" no matter to what uses he leaves the dross which he cannot take with him. Of such as these the public verdict will then be: "The man who dies thus rich dies disgraced."

Such, in my opinion, is the true Gospel concerning Wealth, obedience to which is destined some day to solve the problem of the Rich and the Poor, and to bring "Peace on earth, among men Good Will."
ANDREW CARNEGIE

Riches enlarge, rather than satisfy, appetite. THOMAS FULLER

Many of our rich men have not been content with equal protection and equal benefits but have besought us to make them richer by act of Congress. By attempting to gratify their desires we have in the results of our legislation arrayed section against section, interest against interest, and man against man in a fearful commotion which threatens to shake the foundations of our Union. ANDREW JACKSON

If you look up a dictionary of quotations you will find few reasons for a sensible man to desire to become wealthy. ROBERT LYND

Very few men acquire wealth in such a manner as to receive pleasure from it. As long as there is the enthusiasm of the chase they enjoy it. But when they begin to look around and think of settling down, they find that that part by which joy enters in, is dead to them. They have spent their lives in heaping up colossal piles of treasure, which stand at the end, like pyramids in the desert, holding only the dust of things.

HENRY WARD BEECHER

There is a burden of care in getting riches; fear in keeping them; temptation in using them; guilt in abusing them; sorrow in losing them; and a burden of account at last to be given concerning them.

MATTHEW HENRY

Riches are apt to betray a man into arrogance. JOSEPH ADDISON

There is nothing keeps longer than a middling fortune, and nothing melts away sooner than a great one. Poverty treads on the heels of great and unexpected riches. FREDERICK SAUNDERS

The acquisition of wealth is a work of great labor; its possession a source of continual fear; its loss, of excessive grief. LATIN SAYING

Nothing is so hard for those who abound in riches as to conceive how others can be in want. JONATHAN SWIFT

The richer and bigger you are, the more considerate you have to be of other people's feelings if you are to succeed in taking the curse off being rich. J. OGDON SYMOUR

There never was a banquet so sumptuous but someone dined poorly at it.

FRENCH PROVERB

What has destroyed every previous civilization has been the tendency to the unequal distribution of wealth and power. This same tendency, operating with increasing force, is observable in our civilization today, showing itself in every progressive community, and with greater intensity the more progressive the community. HENRY GEORGE

Golden shackles are far worse than iron ones.

MOHANDUS GHANDHI

Abundance is a blessing to the wise;
The use of riches in discretion lies;
Learn this, ye men of wealth—a heavy purse
In a fool's pocket is a heavy curse. RICHARD CUMBERLAND

They who lie soft and warm in a rich estate seldom come to heat themselves at the altar. ROBERT SOUTH

It is the curse of prosperity that it takes work away from us, and shuts the door to hope and health of spirit. WILLIAM DEAN HOWELLS

Wealth is nothing in itself; it is not useful but when it departs from us; its value is found only in that which it can purchase. As to corporal enjoyment, money can neither open new avenues of pleasure, nor block up the passages of anguish. Disease and infirmity still continue to torture and enfeeble, perhaps exasperated by luxury, or promoted by softness. With respect to the mind, it has rarely been observed that wealth contributes much to quicken the discernment or elevate the imagination, but may, by hiring flattery, or laying diligence asleep, confirm error and harden stupidity. SAMUEL JOHNSON

The problem of our age is the proper administration of wealth so that the ties of brotherhood may still bind together the rich and the poor in harmonious relationships. ANDREW CARNEGIE

What good does this huge weight of gold and silver if fear forces you to bury it secretly in the ground? HORACE

Poverty

The rich are warm, the poor man freezes
And don't let you forget it.
The wealthy eat whene'er it pleases,
The poor when they can get it.

The greatest man in history was the poorest.
RALPH WALDO EMERSON

A rich man is nothing but a poor man with money. W. C. FIELDS

We were so poor, the tooth fairy left I.O.U.'s. ROBERT ORBEN

The chief problem of lower-income farmers is poverty.
NELSON ROCKEFELLER

Poor people have more fun than rich people, they say, and I notice it's the rich people who keep saying it. JACK PAAR

If rich people could hire other people to die for them, the poor could make a wonderful living. YIDDISH PROVERB

God must love the poor, said Lincoln, or he wouldn't have made so many of them. He must love the rich or he wouldn't divide so much mazuma among so few of them. HENRY LOUIS MENCKEN

In one important respect a man is fortunate in being poor. His responsibility to God is so much the less. CHRISTIAN NESTELL BOVEE

There's another advantage of being poor—a doctor will cure you faster. FRANK McKINNEY HUBBARD

For every talent that poverty has stimulated, it has blighted a hundred. JOHN W. GARDNER

Every man has a right to be poor. RICHARD JEFFERIES

There are many of us in this old world of ours who hold that things break about even for all of us. I have observed, for example, that we all get about the same amount of ice. The rich get it in the summer and the poor get it in the winter. BAT MASTERSON

Poverty does not mean the possession of little, but the lack of much. ANTIPATER of MACEDONIA

One of the strangest things about life is that the poor, who need money the most, are the very ones who never have it. FINLEY PETER DUNNE

To be poor and independent is very nearly an impossibility. WILLIAM CORBETT

Poverty is very good in poems, but it is very bad in a house. It is very good in maxims and sermons but it is very bad in practical life. HENRY WARD BEECHER

It's the same the whole world over
Ain't it all a blinking shame,
It's the rich what gets the pleasure
And the poor what gets the blame. ANON

We must all do what we can to save food for the millions who are suffering starvation. JOHN D. ROCKEFELLER

Capital punishment is as fundamentally wrong as a cure for crime as charity is wrong as a cure for poverty. HENRY FORD

If it were not for the holes in the pocket, we should all be rich. A pocket is like a cistern: a small leak at the bottom is worse than a large pump at the top. HENRY WARD BEECHER

The only thing that can console one for being poor is extravagance. OSCAR WILDE

Of all the advantages which come to any young man, I believe it to be demonstrably true that poverty is the greatest. JOSIAH GILBERT HOLLAND

It's no disgrace to be poor, but it might as well be. FRANK McKINNEY HUBBARD

There is only one class in the community that thinks more about money than the rich, and that is the poor. The poor can think of nothing else. That is the misery of being poor. OSCAR WILDE

One cause, which is not always observed, of the insufficiency of riches is that they very seldom make their owner rich. SAMUEL JOHNSON

No man should commend poverty unless he is poor. SAINT BERNARD

Remember the poor—it costs nothing. JOSH BILLINGS

So here is the Great Society. It's the time—and it's going to be soon—when nobody in this country is poor. LYNDON B. JOHNSON

The honest poor can sometimes forget poverty. The honest rich can never forget it. GILBERT KEITH CHESTERTON

It is the weariness of the poor that keeps the rich in power. ANON

Poor men's reasons are not heard. THOMAS FULLER

To be poor and to seem to be poor is a certain way never to rise. OLIVER GOLDSMITH

A person never knows how wonderful it was to be born poor until after he makes money.
ANON

Poverty is taking your children to the hospital and spending the whole day waiting with no one even taking your name—and then coming back the next day, and the next, until they finally get around to you.
MRS. JANICE BRADSHAW

Poverty is no disgrace to a man, but it is confoundly inconvenient.
SYDNEY SMITH

A good poor man is better than a good rich man because he has to resist more temptation.
PLATO

The crying need of the nation is not for better morals, cheaper bread, temperance, liberty, culture, redemption of fallen sisters and erring brothers, not the grace, love, and fellowship of the trinity, but simply for enough money. And the evil to be attacked is not sin, suffering, greed, priestcraft, kingcraft, demagogy, monopoly, ignorance, drink, war, pestilence, nor any of the consequences of poverty, but just poverty itself.
GEORGE BERNARD SHAW

If a free society cannot help the many who are poor, it cannot save the few who are rich.
JOHN F. KENNEDY

The most versatile of all abstractions. . . . Only the poor appreciate the physicality of cash.
KENNETH BAKER

To be a poor man is hard, but to be a poor race in a land of dollars is the very bottom of hardships.
W.E.B. DU BOIS

Our affluent society contains those of talent and insight who are driven to prefer poverty, to choose it, rather than submit to the desolation of an empty abundance.
MICHAEL HARRINGTON

Poverty comes pleading, not for charity, for the most part, but imploring us to find a purchaser for its unmarketable wares.
OLIVER WENDELL HOLMES

The possession of gold has ruined fewer men than the lack of it. What noble enterprises have been checked and what fine souls have been blighted in the gloom of poverty the world will never know.
THOMAS BAILEY ALDRICH

Many a defect is seen in the poor man. IRISH PROVERB

It would be a considerable consolation to the poor and discontented could they but see the means whereby the wealth they covet has been acquired, or the misery that it entails.
JOHANN GEORG ZIMMERMANN

Poverty has many roots, but the top root is ignorance.
LYNDON B. JOHNSON

The poor man is ruined as soon as he begins to ape the rich.
PUBLILIUS SYRUS

Poverty is not a shame, but the being ashamed of it is.
THOMAS FULLER

Poverty often deprives a man of all spirit and virtue; it is hard for an empty bag to stand upright. BENJAMIN FRANKLIN

Ownership

If you lose the lot
Of what you've got,
Your possessions and your houses,
Forget the cost
Of what you've lost,
At least you've got your trousers.

Who has, is. ITALIAN PROVERB

If you don't get everything you want, think of the things you don't get that you don't want. OSCAR WILDE

I want my own fucking country. ROBERT VESCO

I don't want to own anything that won't fit into my coffin. FRED ALLEN

No man can lose what he never had. IZAAK WALTON

Whatever is not nailed down is mine. Whatever I can pry up is not nailed down. COLLIS P. HUNTINGTON

Mine is better than ours. BENJAMIN FRANKLIN

The possession of gold has ruined fewer men than the lack of it. THOMAS BAILEY ALDRICH

Keep a thing seven years and it's bound to come in handy. RUSSIAN PROVERB

The wealthy are indeed rather possessed by their money than possessors. ROBERT BURTON

A man never feels the want of what it never occurs to him to ask for. ARTHUR SCHOPENHAUER

To have a thing is little, if you're not allowed to show it,
And to know a thing is nothing unless others know you know it.
LORD NEAVES

An object in possession seldom retains the same charm that it had in pursuit. PLINY the YOUNGER

The newer people, of this modern age, are more eager to amass than to realize. RABINDZANATH TAGORE

I would rather be able to appreciate things I cannot have than to have things I am not able to appreciate. ELBERT HUBBARD

Everything you have wants to own you. REGINA EILERT

To have may be taken from us, to have had, never. SENECA

To believe that if only we had this or that we would be happy, or to pursue any excessive desire, diverts us from seeing that happiness depends on an adequate self. ERIC HOFFER

Lives based on having are less free than lives based either on doing or on being. WILLIAM JAMES

Riches do not consist in the possession of treasures, but in the use made of them. NAPOLEON BONAPARTE

The possession of a great many things, even the best of things, tends to blind one to the real value of anything. HOLBROOK JACKSON

It is preoccupation with possession, more than anything else, that prevents men from living freely and nobly. BERTRAND RUSSELL

This "I and mine" causes the whole misery. With the sense of possession comes selfishness or thought of selfishness and selfishness brings misery. Every act of selfishness or thought of selfishness makes us attached to something, and immediately we are made slaves. VIVEKANANDA

A pig that has two owners is sure to die of hunger.
ENGLISH PROVERB

Nothing can be so perfect while we possess it as it will seem when remembered. OLIVER WENDELL HOLMES

Possessions, outward success, publicity, luxury—to me these have always been contemptible. I believe that a simple and unassuming manner of life is best for everyone, best both for the body and the mind.
ALBERT EINSTEIN

With the great part of rich people, the chief employment of riches consists in the parade of riches, which, in their eye, is never so complete as when they appear to possess those decisive marks of opulence which nobody can possess but themselves. ADAM SMITH

I glory more in the cunning purchase of my wealth than in the glad possession. BEN JONSON

To pretend to satisfy one's desire by possession is like using straw to put out a fire. CHINESE PROVERB

He that hath nothing is frightened at nothing. THOMAS FULLER

The want of a thing is perplexing enough, but the possession of it is intolerable. JOHN VANBRUGH

The more a man possesses over and above what he uses, the more careworn he becomes. GEORGE BERNARD SHAW

The higher we ascend among human types and the more intense personalities become, the more the importance of possessions dwindles.
VIDA D. SCUDDER

A man can hope for satisfaction and fulfillment only in what he does not yet possess; he cannot find pleasure in something of which he already has too much.
CARL G. JUNG

He who wants a rose must respect the thorn. PERSIAN PROVERB

What we have never had, remains;
It is the things we have that go.
SARA TEASDALE

How sweet an emotion is possession. What charm is inherent in ownership! What a foundation for vanity, even for the greater quality of self-respect, lies in a little property!
DAVID GRAYSON

There is no less merit in keeping what we have got, than in first acquiring it. Chance has something to do with the one, while the other will always be the effect of skill.
OVID

He who possesses most must be most afraid of loss.
LEONARDO da VINCI

Property

When you own a property,
To keep it safe and sure,
The footprint of the owner
Is far the best manure.

The best investment is land, because they ain't making any more of it.
WILL ROGERS

The world seldom asks, how a man acquired his property. The only question is, has he got it?
EDMUND FULLER

It is because property exists that there are wars, riots and injustices.
GRAFFITO

The man who has half a million dollars in property has a much higher interest in the government than the man who has little or no property.
NOAH WEBSTER

When the white man came, we had the land and they had the Bibles; now they have the land and we have the Bibles. DAN GEORGE

The meek shall inherit the earth, but not its mineral rights.
PAUL GETTY

Men honor property above all else. It has the greatest power in human life. EURIPIDES

The system of private property is the most important guarantee of freedom, not only for those who own property but scarcely less for those who do not. FRIEDRICH AUGUST von HAYEK

The thing generally raised on city land is taxes.
CHARLES DUDLEY WARNER

Of all obstacles to that complete democracy of which we dream, is there a greater than property? DAVID GRAYSON

I would rather pay ten million dollars for trademark-goodwill without property than one million dollars for property without trademark-goodwill. GEORGE K. MORROW

Land was never lost for want of an heir. ITALIAN PROVERB

Whoever sells land sells his mother. MEXICAN PROVERB

The great and chief end of men . . . putting themselves under government, is the preservation of their property. JOHN LOCKE

Property is a form of power. SIDNEY HOOK

Few rich men own their own property. The property owns them.
ROBERT G. INGERSOLL

It should be remembered that the foundation of the social contract is property; and its first condition, that every one should be maintained in the peaceful possession of what belongs to him.
JEAN-JACQUES ROSSEAU

If property cannot be abolished, it would be an act of kindness to abolish the poor. EDMUND FULLER

Where all of the man is what property he owns, it does not take long to annihilate him. HENRY WARD BEECHER

The accumulation of property is no guarantee of the development of character, but the development of character, or of any other good whatever, is impossible without property. WILLIAM GRAHAM SUMNER

Ultimately property rights and personal rights are the same thing.
CALVIN COOLIDGE

Wealth in modern societies is distributed according to opportunity; and while opportunity depends partly upon talent and energy, it depends still more upon birth, social position, access to education and inherited wealth: in a word, upon property. R. H. TAWNEY

The world is a fairly untidy place and the most valuable thing one can give to one's children is land. That's the only security.
BERNARD BENSON

Thieves respect property. They merely wish the property to become their property that they may more perfectly respect it.
GILBERT KEITH CHESTERTON

The first farmer was the first man; and all historic nobility rests on possession and use of land. RALPH WALDO EMERSON

The true friend of property, the true conservative is he who insists that property shall be the servant and not the master of the commonwealth; who insists that the creature of man's making shall be the servant and not the master of the man who made it. The citizens of the United States must effectively control the mighty commercial forces which they themselves called into being. THEODORE ROOSEVELT

So soon as the possession of property becomes the basis of popular esteem, therefore, it becomes also a requisite to that complacency which we call self-respect. THORSTEIN VEBLEN

The spirit of property doubles a man's strength.
FRANCOIS VOLTAIRE

Essentially Socialism is no more and no less a criticism of the idea of property in the light of the public good. HERBERT GEORGE WELLS

Property is dear to men not only for the sensual pleasure it can afford, but also because it is the bulwark of all they hold dearest on earth, and above all else, because it is the safeguard of those they love most against misery and all physical distress. WILLIAM GRAHAM SUMNER

Broad acres are a patent of nobility; and no man but feels more of a man in the world if he have a bit of ground that he can call his own. However small it is on the surface, it is four thousand miles deep; and that is a very handsome property. CHARLES DUDLEY WARNER

The rights and interests of the laboring man will be protected and cared for—not by the labor agitators, but by the Christian gentlemen to whom God had given control of the property rights of the country and upon the successful management of which so much depends.

GEORGE F. BAER

The right of private property, the fruit of labor or industry, or of concession or donation by others, is an incontrovertible natural right; and everybody can dispose reasonably of such property as he thinks fit.

OLIVER WENDELL HOLMES

Generosity

Take the "r" out of "free"
And you're left with a "fee,"
Which is what it usually costs you.

Philanthropy is almost the only virtue which is sufficiently appreciated by mankind. HENRY DAVID THOREAU

Nobody who has wealth to distribute ever omits himself.

LEV DAVIDORICH TROTSKY

No McTavish
Was ever lavish. OGDEN NASH

He threw his money about like a man with no arms.
WILLIAM McILVANNEY

I like to be in America!
OK by me in America!
Everything free in America
For a small fee in America!
STEPHEN SONDHEIM

As it is more blessed to give than receive, so it must be more blessed to receive than to give back. ROBERT FROST

It's sweet to be remembered, but it's often cheaper to be forgotten.
FRANK McKINNEY HUBBARD

An optimist is person who thinks he can get by with saying "Thanks" to the head waiter. ANON

I wonder if it ain't just cowardice instead of generosity that makes us give tips. WILL ROGERS

Nobody who has wealth to distribute ever omits himself.
LEON TROTSKY

The great Maimonides once enumerated the various stages of charity, of which the last and most meritorious is to help a man to help himself, to enable him to become self-supporting so that he will no longer have to rely upon the beneficence of others. JACOB M. BRAUDE

Behold, I do not give lectures or a little charity,
When I give I give myself.
WALT WHITMAN

Charity is twice cursed—it hardens him that gives and softens him that takes. BOUCK WHITE

Too many people have decided to do without generosity in order to practice charity. ALBERT CAMUS

Those who give not till they die show that they would not then if they could keep it any longer. JOSEPH HALL

People who are misers with their money often are philanthropists with their troubles. O. A. BATTISTA

Generous? Why that man would give you the sleeves out of his vest!
ANON

Unless a man is a recipient of charity, he should be a contributor to it.
ANON

You give me nothing during your life, but you promise to provide for me at your death. If you are not a fool, you know what you make me wish for.
MARTIAL

All right, so I like spending money! But name one other extravagance!
MAX KAUFFMANN

They asked Jack Benny if he would do something for the Actor's Orphanage—so he shot both his parents and moved in. BOB HOPE

Giving away a fortune is taking Christianity too far.
CHARLOTTE BINGHAM

Plenty of people despise money—few are able to give it away.
DUC de la ROCHEFOUCAULD

It is a gorgeous gold pocket watch. I'm proud of it. My grandfather, on his deathbed, sold me this watch. WOODY ALLEN

When it comes to paying, he's the first to put his hand in his pocket—and leave it there. ANON

Philanthropy is commendable, but it must not cause the philanthropist to overlook the circumstances of economic injustice which make philanthropy necessary. MARTIN LUTHER KING

If rich men would remember that shrouds have no pockets, they would, while living, share their wealth with their children, and give for the good of others, and so know the highest pleasure wealth can give.
TRYON EDWARDS

He that defers his charity until he is dead is, if a man weighs it rightly, rather liberal of another man's goods than his own. FRANCIS BACON

It is but a mean and miserly spirit that for a lifetime keeps wealth only to self, and so leaves children to the struggles of the world without the help that might aid them to comfort and success.
HENRY WADSWORTH LONGFELLOW

Posthumous charities are the very essence of selfishness, when bequeathed by those who, when alive, would part with nothing.
CHARLES CALEB COLTON

Generosity during life is a very different thing from generosity in the hour of death; one proceeds from genuine liberality, and benevolence; the other from pride or fear, or from the fact that you cannot take your money with you to the other world. MARTIAL

III INCOME

Salary

No praise
Repays
A raise.

People who work sitting down get paid more than people who work standing up. OGDEN NASH

When you define a living wage, it depends on whether you are giving or getting it. HERBERT V. PROCHNOW

People who take pains never to do any more than they get paid for, never get paid for any more than they do. ELBERT HUBBARD

The government says two can live on $8,000 a year, but they don't say two what. ANON

He's been there for 25 years and never asked for a raise. That's why he's been there for 25 years. ANON

I've always been worried about people who are willing to work for nothing. Sometimes that's all you get from them, nothing. SAM ERVIN

To double your salary, Xerox your pay check. PAT O'HARE

It is difficult to get a man to understand something when his salary depends upon his not understanding it. UPTON SINCLAIR

Women are getting men's wages now—but then, they always have.
ANON

There is something utterly nauseating about a system of society which pays a harlot 25 times as much as it pays its Prime Minister, 250 times as much as it pays its Members of Parliament, and 500 times as much as it pays some of its ministers of religion. SIR HAROLD WILSON

Give me more money first and then I'll work harder. ANON

The ideal income is a thousand dollars a day—and expenses.
PIERRE LORILLARD

There is nothing more demoralizing than a small but adequate income.
EDMUND WILSON

If you haven't received a raise, ask yourself—not your boss—why.
ANON

A man who received by mistake a pay envelope without a check, asked: "What happened? Did my deductions finally catch up with my salary?"
ANON

We're overpaying him but he's worth it. SAMUEL GOLDWYN

Million dollars: A sum that may be honestly acquired by putting aside five hundred dollars out of one's salary every week for forty years.
ANON

He well remembered that he had a salary to receive, and only forgot that he had a duty to perform. EDWARD GIBBON

One man's wage rise is another man's price increase.
SIR HAROLD WILSON

The salary of the chief executive of the large corporation is not a market award for achievement. It is frequently in the nature of a warm personal gesture by the individual to himself. JOHN KENNETH GALBRAITH

I have always been overpaid to do that which I would pay to do.
PAUL A. SAMUELSON

On being advised not to disclose his salary to anyone the employee concurred with the comment that he was just as much ashamed of it as they were! ANON

Did you hear about the mint employees who went on strike to make less money?
JACK HERBERT

To whom nothing is given, of him can nothing be required.
HENRY FIELDING

We like to keep salaries low so that tax deductions won't be a burden.
DALE McFEATTERS

You can buy a man's time. You can buy a man's physical presence in a given place. You can even buy a measured number of skilled muscular motions per hour or day.

But you cannot buy enthusiasm . . . you cannot buy initiative . . . you cannot buy the devotion of hearts, minds and souls. You have to earn those things.
CLARENCE FRANCIS

What you get is a living—what you give is a life.
LILIAN GISH

A motto to express the ideal of maximum service and efficiency: "Make sure you are underpaid."
V. ORVAL WATTS

Featherbedding is the practice of doing less, having more time to do it in, and getting more pay for not doing it.
EVAN ESAR

How much a man is paid usually depends on how many people he can get to do a job as well as if he did it himself.
O. A. BATTISTA

A man properly must pay the fiddler. In my case it so happened that a whole symphony orchestra often had to be subsidized.
JOHN BARRYMORE

There are few sorrows, however poignant, in which a good income is of no avail.
LOGAN PEARSALL SMITH

It is better to have a permanent income than to be fascinating.
OSCAR WILDE

Wages are the measure of dignity that society puts on a job.
JOHNNIE TILLMON

Be content with your wages.
Luke

If you pay not a servant his wages, he will pay himself.
PROVERB

Remuneration? O! That's the Latin word for three farthings.
WILLIAM SHAKESPEARE

The first consideration for all, throughout life, is the earning of a living.
IHARA JAIKUKU

Income is the natural and rational gauge of respectability.
AMBROSE BIERCE

Living on Income

Nowadays it's quite a feat
If you can make just one end meet.

Just about the time you think you can make both ends meet, somebody moves the ends.
PANSY PENNER

The man who drives this year's car on next year's income is probably wearing last year's clothes.
EVAN ESAR

I hope they don't raise the standard of living any higher, I can't afford it now.
MAT WEINSTOCK

The next time you call your dog a dumb animal, remember who he's got working to support him.
ANON

Maybe they call it take-home pay because there is no other place you can afford to go with it.
FRANKLIN P. JONES

Blue Cross is a company that docks my pay to pay my doc.
ANON

I'm on a low-salary diet.
ROBERT TEMPLE

An income is what you can't live without or within.
ANON

Income is something to live beyond.
ANON

There are several ways in which to apportion the family income, all of them unsatisfactory.
ROBERT BENCHLEY

We want inflation of our income and deflation of everything else.
ANON

I'm living so far beyond my income that we may almost be said to be living apart.
H. H. MUNRO

Nowadays, if you miss a day's work, the government loses as much as you do.
ANON

Live beyond your means; then you're forced to work hard—you have to succeed.
EDWARD G. ROBINSON

Years ago I used to dream about getting the salary I'm now starving on.
ANON

The man I am sorry for is the man who goes through life without any invisible means of support.
J. TUDOR REES

The kind of fallout that really disturbs most citizens is what gets dropped out of their pay checks.
ANON

Keeping up with the Joneses was a full-time job with my mother and father. It was not until many years later that, when I lived alone, I realized how much cheaper it was to drag the Joneses down to my level.
QUENTIN CRISP

America is a great country, but you can't live in it for nothing.
WILL ROGERS

Annual income twenty pounds, annual expenditure nineteen nineteen six, result happiness. Annual income twenty pounds, annual expenditure twenty pounds ought and six, result misery.
CHARLES DICKENS

Let us live within our income, even if we have to borrow the money to do it.
ARTEMUS WARD

The larger the income, the harder it is to live within it.
ARCHBISHOP RICHARD WHATELY

Expenditure rises to meet income. Individual expenditure not only rises to meet income but tends to surpass it.
C. NORTHCOTE PARKINSON

The secret of economy is to live as cheaply the first few days after payday as you lived the last few days before.
ANON

He is rich whose income is more than his expenses; and he is poor whose expenses exceed his income. JEAN de la BRUYÈRE

Almost any man knows how to earn money, but not one in a million knows how to spend it. If he had known so much as this, he would never have earned it. HENRY DAVID THOREAU

We do not desire money for itself but for what it will bring us by way of the luxuries of life. ANON

Our incomes are like our shoes; if too small, they gall and pinch us; but if too large, they cause us to stumble and trip.
CHARLES CALEB COLTON

The art of living easily as to money is to pitch your scale of living one degree below your means. SIR HENRY TAYLOR

He who is taught to live upon little owes more to his father's wisdom than he that has a great deal left him does to his father's care.
WILLIAM PENN

There is no sense in attempting to fit into a ready-to-wear financial pattern which ignores your own personal wants and desires.
SYLVIA PORTER

I am indeed rich since my income is superior to my expense, and my expense is equal to my wishes. EDWARD GIBBON

Make all you can, save all you can, give all you can. JOHN WESLEY

People's spending habits depend more on how wealthy they feel than with the actual amount of their current income. A. C. PIGOU

Cash

Dollars don't fall from heaven,
When there is a bucket.
When dollars do fall from heaven
Aah! Forget it!

I wish they wouldn't keep referring to the American dollar as stable. You know what's found in stables. ROBERT ORBEN

You show me how to put two million dollars in a suitcase and I'll give you the two million dollars. FRANK SINATRA

What this country needs is a good five cent nickel. ED WYNN

A nickel ain't worth a dime anymore. YOGI BERRA

No man is a hero to his wallet. ANON

A good many foreigners think the eagle on the American dollar is the bird of paradise. ANON

Yesterday is a cancelled check; tomorrow is a promissory note; today is ready cash—use it. KAY LYONS

Size is no indication of value. A ten dollar bill is no larger than a one dollar bill. ANON

There's nothing so comfortable as a small bankroll. A big one is always in danger. WILSON MIZNER

One coin that you have is worth more than five you hope for.
JEAN de la FONTAINE

He who does not accept cash when offered is no businessman.
CHINESE PROVERB

You never own a coin. You only have life tenancy on it. You hold it, study it, appreciate it. It goes on to others after you to do the same.
EDWARD JANIS

There are three faithful friends—an old wife, an old dog, and ready money. BENJAMIN FRANKLIN

A penny will hide the biggest star in the universe if you hold it close enough to your eye. SAMUEL GRAFTON

Pounds are the sons, not of pounds, but of pence. CHARLES BUXTON

My life is a bubble, but how much solid cash it costs to keep that bubble floating! LOGAN PEARSALL SMITH

'Tis ready money makes the man. WILLIAM SOMERVILLE

Nowhere more naively than in bank-notes does capitalism display itself in solemn earnest. The innocent cupids frolicking about numbers: the goddesses holding tablets of the law: the stalwart heroes sheathing their swords before monetary units are a world of their own ornamenting the facade of hell. WALTER BENJAMIN

Everyone, even the richest and most munificent of men, pays much by check more lightheartedly than he pays little in specie.
MAX BEERBOHM

Cost

Blow the cost,
Take what comes;
You'll be lost
With the bums.

You ladies know that if you stand in front of the asparagus counter at the supermarket these days, it's cheaper to eat money.
RONALD REAGAN

Money often costs too much. RALPH WALDO EMERSON

A thing of beauty is a great expense. ANON

I haven't heard of anybody who wants to stop living on account of the cost. FRANK McKINNEY HUBBARD

These days when you eat out at a fancy restaurant, you need an after dinner mint—like the one in Denver. ANON

Who recalls when folks got along without something if it cost too much?
FRANK McKINNEY HUBBARD

What costs nothing is worth nothing. ANON

A man is a person who will pay two dollars for a one-dollar item he wants. A woman will pay one dollar for a two-dollar item she doesn't want. WILLIAM BINGER

Too caustic? To hell with the cost, we'll make the picture anyway.
SAMUEL GOLDWYN

There are plenty of good five-cent cigars in the country. The trouble is, they cost a quarter. FRANKLIN PIERCE ADAMS

I think some folks are foolish to pay what it costs to live.
FRANK McKINNEY HUBBARD

If you don't believe lead can be changed into gold, wait till you get a bill from your plumber. *Good Reading*

You can't get anything without paying for it.
BOSS WILLIAM MARCY TWEED

One of the difficult tasks in this world is to convince a woman that even a bargain costs money. EDGAR WATSON HOWE

What you get free costs too much. JEAN ANOUILH

That man is richest whose pleasures are the cheapest.
HENRY DAVID THOREAU

Price

The price is never right to buy;
It always has and will be so.
To the buyer it is much too high,
And to the seller much too low.

Every time history repeats itself, the price goes up. ANON

It makes no difference what it is, a woman will buy anything she thinks the store is losing money on. FRANK McKINNEY HUBBARD

Buy something today, and tomorrow someone could have got it for you cheaper. ROYSTON DURSLEY

A fair price for oil is whatever you can get plus ten per cent.
DR. ALI' AHMED ATTIGA

A grocer was asked why his prices were always higher at weekends. He replied, "They aren't higher at weekends, they're lower during the week."
ANON

When you buy something for a song, you may have to face the music later on.
RAYMOND CVIKOTA

Bargain: something you can't use at a price you can't resist.
FRANKLIN P. JONES

The way production costs are soaring, the fellow who used "to get it wholesale" now can buy it cheaper abroad.
ANON

There is a Spanish proverb that one who would grow rich must buy of those who go to be executed, as not caring how cheap they sell; and sell to those who go to be married as not caring how dear they buy.
THOMAS FULLER

Price is what you pay; value is what you receive.
ANON

A cynic is a man who knows the price of everything and the value of nothing.
OSCAR WILDE

Everything is worth what its purchaser will pay for it.
ALBERT EINSTEIN

What is a man if he is not a thief who openly charges as much as he can for the goods he sells.
MOHANDAS K. GANDHI

Good bargains empty our pockets.
GERMAN PROVERB

The best is the cheapest.
BENJAMIN FRANKLIN

He will never get a good thing cheap that is afraid to ask the price.
ANON

Nothing is to be had for nothing.
EPICTETUS

Cheat me in the price but not in the goods.
THOMAS FULLER

The highest price we can pay for anything is to ask it.
WALTER SAVAGE LANDOR

The real price of everything, what everything really costs to the man who wants to acquire it, is the toil and trouble of acquiring it.

ADAM SMITH

A man often pays dear for a small frugality.

RALPH WALDO EMERSON

The "value" or "worth" of a man is, as of all other things, his price; that is to say, so much as would be given for the use of his power.

THOMAS HOBBES

All good things are cheap; all bad are very dear.

HENRY DAVID THOREAU

Of all speculations the market holds forth,
  The best that I know for a lover of pelf
Is to buy Marcus up, at the price he is worth,
  And then sell him at that which he sets on himself.

THOMAS MOORE

What we think an unreasonable price when we are to buy, we think just and equitable when we are to sell. ANON

Never buy what you do not want because it is cheap; it will be dear to you. THOMAS JEFFERSON

Buy not what you want, but what you have need of; what you do not want is dear at a farthing. CATO the CENSOR

Self-respect is a question of recognizing that anything worth having has its price. JOAN DIDION

Value

If you buy something exceedingly cheap,
Try to find someone who's always asleep.
Make a quick profit,
Take your cut off it,
'Cos it's probably not worth it to keep.

We never know the worth of water till the well is dry.

THOMAS FULLER

It's a terribly hard job to spend a billion dollars and get your money's worth. GEORGE HUMPHREY

Men go shopping just as men go out fishing or hunting, to see how large a fish may be caught with the smallest hook. HENRY WARD BEECHER

Everything is worth what its purchaser will pay for it.
PUBLILIUS SYRUS

In the old days, $10 worth of groceries would fill a pantry to bursting. Today, $10 worth of groceries won't even burst a shopping bag. Certainly shows how much stronger bags are now, doesn't it? DAVID SAVAGE

Buy Old Masters. They fetch a much better price than old mistresses.
LORD BEAVERBROOK

America: The country where you buy a lifetime supply of aspirin for one dollar, and use it up in two weeks. JOHN BARRYMORE

The value of anything is not what you paid for it, not what it cost to produce, but what you can get for it at an auction.
WILLIAM LYON PHELPS

We have just heard of a lifetime guarantee that is valid for three months.
ANON

An indispensable thing never has much value.
RUSSIAN PROVERB

The urge to consume is fathered by the value system which emphasizes the ability of the society to produce. JOHN KENNETH GALBRAITH

Things are only worth what you make them worth.
JEAN-BAPTISTE MOLIÈRE

The value of a man can only be measured with regard to other men.
FRIEDRICH WILHELM NIETZSCHE

If you buy cheap meat, when it boils you smell what you have saved.
ARABIAN PROVERB

The timid man yearns for full value and demands a tenth. The bold man strikes for double value and compromises on par. MARK TWAIN

We often despise what is most useful to us. AESOP

People who want something for nothing are life's suckers.
MEYER LANSKY

What is valuable is not new, and what is new is not valuable.
DANIEL WEBSTER

Never buy a thing you don't want merely because it is dear.
OSCAR WILDE

Try not to become a man of success but rather to become a man of value.
ALBERT EINSTEIN

Less is only more where more is no good. FRANK LLOYD WRIGHT

What is good to take, is good to keep. FRENCH PROVERB

Men insisted that the true standard of value was the kilowatt-hour.
SENATOR ROBERT OWEN

What is bought is cheaper than a gift. PORTUGUESE PROVERB

Surely there comes a time when counting the cost and paying the price aren't things to think about any more. All that matters is value—the ultimate value of what one does. JAMES HILTON

What's got badly, goes badly. IRISH PROVERB

Nothing seems to me of the smallest value except what one gets out of oneself. OSCAR WILDE

Prosperity has everything cheap. THOMAS FULLER

There is no such thing as absolute value in this world. You can only estimate what a thing is worth to you. CHARLES DUDLEY WARNER

Strongly spent is synonymous with kept. ROBERT FROST

Today's egg is better than tomorrow's hen. TURKISH PROVERB

For what is worth in anything but so much money as 'twill bring?
SAMUEL BUTLER

A poor man's roast and a rich man's death are sniffed far off.
YIDDISH PROVERB

A cloak is not made for a single shower of rain. ITALIAN PROVERB

What we obtain too cheap, we esteem too lightly; it is dearness only that gives everything its value. THOMAS PAINE

Nothing is cheap which is superfluous, for what one does not need, is dear at a penny. PLUTARCH

Saving

Money saved is money earned;
There's nothing less perverser.
It is true when it is learned,
But seldom vice versa.

If you want to know whether you are destined to be a success or a failure in life, you can easily find out. The test is simple and it is infallible. Are you able to save money? If not, drop out. You will lose. You may not think so, but you will lose, as sure as you live. The seed of success is not in you. JAMES J. HILL

When a man begins to think seriously of saving for a rainy day, it's probably a rainy day. ANON

When one has had to work so hard to get money, why should he impose on himself the further hardship of trying to save it? DON HEROLD

Everyone should save because spending costs money. ANON

Simply by not owning three medium-sized castles in Tuscany I have saved enough money in the last forty years on insurance premiums alone to buy a medium-sized castle in Tuscany. GEORGE MIKES

Jesus saves—today he's the only one who can afford to. GRAFFITO

A dollar saved is a quarter earned. JOHN CIARDI

The greatest waste of money is to keep it. JACKIE GLEASON

In this world, it is not what we take up, but what we give up, that makes us rich. HENRY WARD BEECHER

Old men are always advising young men to save money. That is bad advice. Don't save every nickel. Invest in yourself. I never saved a dollar until I was 40 years old. HENRY FORD

There is no profit in going to bed early to save candles if the result is twins. ANON

If a man saves $15 a week and invests in good common stocks and allows the dividends and rights to accumulate, at the end of 20 years he will have at least $80,000. He will have an income from investments of around $400 a month. JOHN J. RASKOB

Any young man with good health and a poor appetite can save up money. JAMES MONTGOMERY BAILEY

A man may, if he knows not how to save as he gets, keep his nose all his life to the grindstone, and die not worth a groat after all. BENJAMIN FRANKLIN

To recommend thrift to the poor is like advising a man who is starving to eat less. OSCAR WILDE

I find it more trouble to take care of money than to get it. MICHEL de MONTAIGNE

Get what you can and keep what you have, that's the way to get rich. SCOTTISH PROVERB

The petty economies of the rich are just as amazing as the silly extravagances of the poor. WILLIAM FEATHER

Men who make money rarely saunter; men who save money rarely swagger. EDWARD BULWER-LYTTON

In the old days a man who saved money was a miser; now he is a wonder. ANON

A miser grows rich by seeming poor; an extravagant man grows poor by seeming rich. WILLIAM SHAKESPEARE

Oh, I wish I were a miser; being a miser is so occupying. GERTRUDE STEIN

The farmer's way of saving money: to be owed by someone he trusted.
HUGH MacLENNAN

Men are divided between those who are as thrifty as if they would live forever, and those who are as extravagant as if they were going to die the next day.
ARISTOTLE

It's no use filling your pocket with money if you have a hole in the corner.
GEORGE ELIOT

The secret of making money is saving it. It is not what a man earns—not the amount of his income, but the relation of his expenditure to his receipts, that determines his poverty or wealth.
CHARLES CALEB COLTON

Every miser has a spendthrift son.
FRENCH PROVERB

A man who both spends and saves money is the happiest man, because he has both enjoyments.
SAMUEL JOHNSON

A penny saved is a penny to squander.
AMBROSE BIERCE

There is nothing in saving money. The thing to do with it is to put it back into yourself, into your work, into the thing that is important, into whatever you are so much interested in that it is more important than money.
HENRY FORD

As an occupation in declining years, I declare I think saving is useful, amusing and not unbecoming. It must be a perpetual amusement. It is a game that can be played by day, by night, at home and abroad, and at which you must win in the long run. What an interest it imparts to life!
WILLIAM M. THACKERAY

Penny and penny,
Laid up will be many.
ANON

If a man empties his purse into his head, no one takes it from him.
BENJAMIN FRANKLIN

Give me some kind of content to remember how painful it is sometimes to keep money, as well as to get it.
SAMUEL PEPYS

Not to be covetous is money in your purse; not to be eager to buy is income
CICERO

IV FINANCE

Finance

The more you have,
The more you need.

Finance is the art of passing currency from hand to hand until it finally disappears. ROBERT W. SARNOFF

High finance isn't burglary or obtaining money by false pretenses, but rather a judicious selection from the best features of those fine arts.
FINLEY PETER DUNNE

Only one fellow in ten thousand understands the currency question, and we meet him every day. KIN HUBBARD

If Switzerland didn't exist, the financial world would have to invent it.
FINANCIAL AXIOM

Finance is the art of borrowing on the strength of what you already owe.
ANON

Why do they call it a floating pound when all it does is sink?
RAVI TIKKOO

These heroes of finance are like beads on a string—when one slips off, all the rest follow. HENRIK IBSEN

And furthermore did you know that behind the discovery of America there was a Jewish financier? MORDECAI RICHLER

Jesus saves.
—Moses invests.
—Onan spends. GRAFFITO

Gold is a metal men dig out of holes for dentists and government to put back in. ANON

A financier is a pawnbroker with imagination. SIR ARTHUR PINERO

The way to stop financial "joy-riding" is to arrest the chauffeur, not the automobile. THOMAS WOODROW WILSON

Rags make paper,
Paper makes money,
Money makes banks,
Banks make loans,
Loans make beggars,
Beggars make rags. ANON

Never give beyond the possibility of return. BALTASAR GRACIAN

Financier's telegram: WIRE ME HOW CASE CAME OUT.
Lawyer's telegram: RIGHT HAS TRIUMPHED.
Financier's telegram: APPEAL IMMEDIATELY.
GERALD F. LIEBERMAN

Americans want action for their money. They are fascinated by its self-producing qualities if it's put to work. . . . Gold-hoarding goes against the American grain; it fits in better with European pessimism than with America's traditional optimism. PAULA NELSON

When you see a situation you cannot understand, look for the financial interest. TOM L. JOHNSON

The faults of the burglar are the qualities of the financier.
GEORGE BERNARD SHAW

I finally know what distinguishes man from other beasts: financial worries. JULES RENARD

The saddest story I ever heard was about a businessman who was on the brink of bankruptcy. Seeking solace, he turned to his copy of the Good Book, opened it at random, and the first thing he saw was Chapter Eleven. ROBERT ORBEN

Financial sense is knowing that certain men will promise to do certain things, and fail. EDGAR WATSON HOWE

Tomorrow is a post-dated cheque.
Today is cash. *The Irish Digest*

If all men were rational, all politicians honest and we had a world central bank issuing a single currency that was universally acceptable, then gold would drop to $20 an ounce—and be overvalued at that.
ANDRE SHARON

In financial matters, no decision is often better than a hasty decision.
WILLIAM FEATHER

Subsidy: a formula for handing you back your own money with a flourish that makes you think it's a gift. JO BINGHAM

Nobody is a gentleman when big money is involved. JOHN LEONARD

More than one pessimist got that way by financing an optimist.
FRED W. BRENDER

When one optimist finances another optimist, guess which one becomes a pessimist? EVAN ESAR

The world is a pleasanter place when there are low gold prices. Low gold prices signify trust and friendship. HENRY JARECKI

We have heard it said that five per cent is the natural interest of money.
THOMAS MACAULAY

The elegant simplicity of the three per cents. LORD STOWELL

There seems to be a Gresham's Law in cultural as well as monetary circulation: bad stuff drives out the good, it is more easily understood and enjoyed. DWIGHT MacDONALD

Whatever you can lose, reckon of no account. PUBLILIUS SYRUS

Profit

Look at profit's true role
As one of your bosses;
It sure meets the payroll
Much better than losses.

The only real gauge of success we have is profit—honest profit.
REX BEACH

The next guy who talks to me about tonnage is going to get his salary in tons, and we'll see how he converts that into dollars. JOHN C. LOBB

Profits are part of the mechanism by which society decides what it wants to see produced. HENRY C. WALLICH

Volume times zero isn't too healthy. LEE IACOCCA

It is not from the benevolence of the butcher, the brewer, or the baker that we expect our dinner, but from their regard to their own interest.
ADAM SMITH

The only way to keep score in business is to add up how much money you make. HARRY B. HELMSLEY

Little by little, the pimps have taken over the world. They don't do anything, they don't make anything—they just stand there and take their cut. JEAN GIRAUDOUX

If profits are evil, losses must be ten times worse. ANON

The smell of profit is clean and sweet, whatever the source.
DECIMUS JUNIUS JUVENAL

No man can be said to be making too much profit if many others are trying to beat him at his own game, and none can succeed. The larger his profit, the greater will be the number of those who will try and the greater the chance that they will succeed. CLARENCE B. RANDALL

More men come to doom through dirty profits than are kept by them.
SOPHOCLES

There are no gains without pains. ADLAI STEVENSON

If one has not made a reasonable profit, one has made a mistake. LI XIANNIAN

It is well known what a middle-man is: he is the man who bamboozles one party and plunders the other. BENJAMIN DISRAELI

The trouble with the profit system has always been that it was highly unprofitable to most people. ELWYN BROOKS WHITE

The worst crime against working people is a company which fails to operate at a profit. SAMUEL GOMPERS

Zoologist Desmond Morris once did an experiment that exposed an ape to the "profit motive." First of all he got it to draw and paint, and found that it was doing lovely things. Then he started rewarding the ape with peanuts for its work.

"Soon it was doing any old scrawl to get the peanuts," Morris said wryly. "I had introduced commercialism into the ape's world, and ruined him as an artist!" THOMAS WISEMAN

The percentage of student activists who regard business as overly concerned with profits as against social responsibility has increased sharply in just one year. JOHN D. ROCKEFELLER

Profitability is the sovereign criterion of the enterprise. PETER F. DRUCKER

Profits are not bedfellows of honor. TAYLOR CALDWELL

We all have our eyes on the amount of our profits—but one good way to increase them is to watch the percentage of profit. The relation of profits to the selling price—and to your investment—is the real index of business success. LESTER WITTE

There are occasions when it is undoubtedly better to incur loss than to make gain. TITUS MACCIUS PLAUTUS

Even genius is tied to profit. PINDAR

If you don't profit from your investment mistakes, someone else will. YALE HIRSCH

Prefer a loss to a dishonest gain: the one brings pain at the moment, the other for all time.
CHILON

Losing potential profits hurts the ego; losing money really hurts.
GERALD APPEL

I believe in profit sharing—I believe it will ultimately settle the labor problem.
CHARLES M. SCHWAB

Civilization and profits go hand in hand.
CALVIN COOLIDGE

Most of the occasional nonsense written in this country to decry the profit motive is either ignorance or hypocrisy; it either is failure to understand the importance of self-interest in increasing the total wealth of all of the people, or just plain shutting of the eyes to the truth. For myself, I have never known a man who did not at times seek to advance his own self-interest.
CLARENCE B. RANDALL

A business with an income at its heels
Furnishes always oil for its own wheels.
WILLIAM COWPER

Light gains make heavy purses.
ENGLISH PROVERB

The society of excess profits for some and small returns for others, the society in which a few prey upon the many, the society in which a few took great advantage and many took great disadvantage must pass.
WENDELL L. WILKIE

Capital

When anyone has overspent
And finds himself in excrement,
Reaction is to some extent
Future capital punishment.

Capital is past savings accumulated for future production.
JACKSON MARTINDELL

A criminal is a person with predatory instincts who has not sufficient capital to form a corporation.
HOWARD SCOTT

Spending one's capital is feeding a dog on his own tail. MARK TWAIN

The difference between a little money and no money at all is enormous—and can shatter the world. And the difference between a little money and an enormous amount of money is very slight—and that, also, can shatter the world. THORNTON WILDER

All my available funds are completely tied up in ready cash.
W. C. FIELDS

Mud with a little gold in it is often more highly prized than gold with a little mud on it. EDMUND FULLER

Only a profitable business can generate or raise the capital that will enable it to grow, produce more goods, hire more people, and pay improving wages. FREDERICK R. KAPPEL

Capital formation is shifting from the entrepreneur who invests in the future to the pension trustee who invests in the past.
PETER F. DRUCKER

I don't commit any capital. I just make it. ALBERT R. BROCCOLI

I've got some liquid assets—two bottles of whiskey.
LEOPOLD FECHTNER

Capital is that part of wealth which is devoted to obtaining further wealth. ALFRED MARSHALL

You cannot take a whiff of "Free enterprise" or a "Way of Life" and start a factory with it. To start a factory and provide jobs, you have to have money—capital. ERIC JOHNSTON

We cannot eat the fruit while the tree is in blossom.
BENJAMIN DISRAELI

Without big business great accumulations of capital cannot be mobilized from investors to buy the tools and equipment necessary for technological advance and a reduction in the price of goods to the people.
MARGARET CHASE SMITH

Some men worship rank, some worship heroes, some worship power, some worship God, and over these ideals they dispute—but they all worship money. MARK TWAIN

Parsimony, and not industry, is the immediate cause of the increase of capital. Industry, indeed, provides the subject which parsimony accumulates. But whatever industry might acquire, if parsimony did not save and store up, the capital would never be the greater. ADAM SMITH

That men who are industrious and sober and honest in the pursuit of their own interests should after a while accumulate capital, and after that should be allowed to enjoy it in peace, and also if they should choose, when they have accumulated it, to use it to save themselves from actual labor, and hire other people to labor for them, is right. In doing so, they do not wrong the men they employ, for they find men who have not their own land to work upon, or shops to work in, and who are benefited by working for others—hired laborers, receiving their capital for it. Thus a few men that own capital hire a few others, and these establish the relation of capital and labor rightfully—a relation of which I make no complaint. ABRAHAM LINCOLN

Practices of the unscrupulous money changers stand indicted in the court of public opinion, rejected by the hearts and minds of men. . . . The money changers have fled from their high seats in the temple of our civilization. We may now restore the temple to the ancient truths. FRANKLIN D. ROOSEVELT

Credit

Credit is the worst distorter
A contracter and prolonger.
Every month seems to get shorter
And every year much longer.

Credit is something vastly inferior to money. MAX GRALNICK

No man's credit is as good as his money. EDGAR WATSON HOWE

Creditors have better memories than debtors. BENJAMIN FRANKLIN

Credit: a person who can't pay, gets another person who can't pay, to guarantee that he can pay. CHARLES DICKENS

The only reason a great many American families don't own an elephant is that they have never been offered an elephant for a dollar down and easy weekly payments. JACOB M. BRAUDE

Never in the history of human credit has so much been owed.
MARGARET THATCHER

A preferential creditor is the first person to be told there's no money left.
ANON

We have a special arrangement with the bank. They don't serve food, we don't cash checks. MENU POSTCRIPT

The only thing to buy on credit is your casket. JAMES A. MICHENER

How can the auto business make money out of something nobody has paid for? ANON

If a feller screwed up his face when he asked for credit like he does when he's asked t'settle, he wouldn't git it. FRANK McKINNEY HUBBARD

No man is impatient with his creditors. *The Talmud*

Credit is like chastity, they can both stand temptation better than suspicion. JOSH BILLINGS

If you don't want prosperity to falter, then Buy, Buy, Buy—on credit, of course. In other words, the surest way of bringing on a rainy day is to prepare for it. JOSEPH WOOD KRUTCH

A debtor is a man who owes money and a creditor is the man who thinks he's going to get it. ANON

I would gladly pay you Tuesday for a hamburger today.
J. WELLINGTON WIMPY

A luxury becomes a necessity if you can make the down payment on it.
HERBERT V. PROCHNOW

That most delicious of all privileges—spending other people's money.
JOHN RANDOLPH

Some people say a front-engine car handles best. Some people say a rear-engine car handles best. I say a rented car handles best.

P. J. O'ROURKE

Credit is the only enduring testimonial to man's confidence in man.

JAMES BLISH

Endorsing character is hazardous; endorsing credit, presumptuous.

CHARLES SIMMONS

Let us live in as small a circle as we will, we are either debtors or creditors before we have had time to look round.

JOHANN WOLFGANG von GOETHE

Creditors are a superstitious sect, great observers of set days and times.

BENJAMIN FRANKLIN

A pig bought on credit is forever grunting. SPANISH PROVERB

Credit is not only one of the main pillars of the public safety, it is among the principal engines of useful enterprises and internal improvement. As a substitute for capital, it is a little less useful than gold or silver.

ALEXANDER HAMILTON

A creditor is worse than a master—for a master owns only your person—a creditor owns your dignity and can belabor that.

VICTOR HUGO

However gradual may be the growth of confidence, that of credit requires still more time to arrive at maturity. BENJAMIN DISRAELI

Ah, take the Cash, and let the Credit go
Nor heed the rumble of a distant Drum! OMAR KHAYYAM

Credit is the capital of a younger son, and he can live charmingly on it.

OSCAR WILDE

Credit, like a looking glass,
Broken once, is gone, alas! ANON

As a very important source of strength and security, cherish public credit, as one method of preserving it is to use it as sparingly as possible, avoiding occasions of expense by cultivating peace.

GEORGE WASHINGTON

Debt

With payments from a debtor,
When they start to fake it,
It's always so much better
To break the stake and take it.

Only Americans have mastered the art of being prosperous though broke. KELLY FORDYCE

There are more ways of getting into debt than there are of paying it off. ANON

You are not in debt, Sextus. I assure you, Sextus, you are not in debt, for a man is in debt, Sextus, only if he can pay. MARTIAL

There is no contentment as great as being completely free of debt. ANON

We often pay our debts, not because it is only fair that we should, but to make future loans easier. FRANCOIS DUC de la ROCHEFOUCAULD

He who hesitates to pay his bills is soon reminded. ANON

At the celebration of the Chinese New Year, one of the most honored observations is that of paying off all old debts. And we send missionaries to China! ANON

Some people use half their ingenuity to get into debt, and the other half to avoid paying it. GEORGE D. PRENTICE

The two most beautiful words in the English language are: "Check enclosed" DOROTHY PARKER

We pay the debts of the last generation by issuing bonds payable by the next generation. LAWRENCE J. PETER

Time is money and many people pay their debts with it. JOSH BILLINGS

First payments is what made us think we were prosperous, and the other nineteen is what showed us we were broke. WILL ROGERS

Lend me $1,000 and I'll always be indebted to you. ANON

Words pay no debts. WILLIAM SHAKESPEARE

If you don't settle your account, I will tell all your other creditors that you did! ANON

If I owe Smith ten dollars, and God forgives me, that doesn't pay Smith. ROBERT GREEN INGERSOLL

Some pay before due
Some pay when due
Some pay when past due
Some never do
How do you do? ANON

If it isn't the sheriff, it's the finance company. I've got more attachments on me than a vacuum cleaner. JOHN BARRYMORE

God forbid that I should be out of debt as if, indeed, I could not be trusted. FRANÇOIS RABELAIS

A debt is the only thing that does not become smaller when it's contracted. ANON

No debt ever comes due at a good time, yet borrowing is the only thing that's handy all the time. WILL ROGERS

Never run into debt, not if you can find anything else to run into. JOSH BILLINGS

The most important question in this country today, "How much is the down payment?" ANON

Debts are like children: the smaller they are the more noise they make. SPANISH PROVERB

Isn't it frightening how soon later comes, after you buy now? EARL WILSON

"Did you get the check I sent you?"
"Twice—once from you and once from the bank."
LEOPOLD FECHTNER

A small debt produces a debtor; a large one, an enemy.
PUBLILIUS SYRUS

Be back next Thursday and bring a specimen of your money.
GROUCHO MARX

In the midst of life we are in debt. ETHEL WATTS MUMFORD

Did you hear about the fellow who was so far in debt he became a collector's item? BLACKIE SHERROD

He that payeth beforehand shall have his work ill done.
THOMAS FULLER

When some men discharge an obligation you can hear the report for miles around. MARK TWAIN

Debts are nowadays like children, begot with pleasure, but brought forth with pain. JEAN BAPTISTE MOLIÈRE

He that pays last never pays twice. ENGLISH PROVERB

Debts shorten life. JOSEPH JOUBERT

Interest works night and day, in fair weather and in foul. It gnaws at a man's substance with invisible teeth. HENRY WARD BEECHER

A good grievance is better than bad payment. SPANISH PROVERB

A poor man's debt makes a great noise. THOMAS FULLER

That is but an empty purse that is full of other men's money.
PROVERB

It is a sure sign of an improved character, if you like paying debts as much as getting money. GEORG C. LICHTENBERG

Debt is a trap which a man sets and baits himself, and then deliberately gets into. JOSH BILLINGS

Say nothing of my debts unless you mean to pay them.
SPANISH PROVERB

I am not sure just what the unpardonable sin is, but I believe it is a disposition to evade the payment of small bills. ELBERT HUBBARD

Home life ceases to be free and beautiful as soon as it is founded on borrowing and debt. HENRIK JOHAN IBSEN

Take from the bad debtor, even if it is only a stone.
ARABIAN PROVERB

The two greatest stimulants in the world are youth and debt
BENJAMIN DISRAELI

Small debts are like smallshot; they are rattling on every side, and can scarcely be escaped without a wound; great debts are like cannon; of loud noise, but little danger. SAMUEL JOHNSON

You know it is not my Interest to pay the Principal; nor is it my Principle to pay the Interest RICHARD BRINSLEY SHERIDAN

Always pay: for first or last you must pay your entire debt.
RALPH WALDO EMERSON

His brow is wet with honest sweat,
He earns whate'er he can,
And looks the whole world in the face,
For he owes not any man. HENRY WADSWORTH LONGFELLOW

Loans

The amount you repay
Is viewed with much sorrow;
So much larger, some way,
Than the sum that you borrow.

I should describe the human race as a strange species of bipeds who cannot run fast enough to collect the money which they owe themselves.
DONALD ROBERT PERRY MARQUIS

When a man needs money, he needs money, and not a headache tablet or a prayer. WILLIAM FEATHER

It's better to give than to lend and it costs about the same.
SIR PHILIP GIBBS

Loans are month to month resuscitation. FRANKLIN JONES

Pawnbrokers survive on the flat of the land. ANON

It saves a lot of trouble if, instead of having to earn money and save it, you can just go and borrow it. SIR WINSTON CHURCHILL

If you want the time to pass quickly, just give your note for ninety days.
ROBERT BAILEY THOMAS

The person who says No is more likely to have money than the one who says Yes. ANON

To borrow money, big money, you have to wear your clothes in a certain way, walk in a certain way, and have about you an air of solemnity and majesty something like the atmosphere of a Gothic cathedral.
STEPHEN LEACOCK

A good loan is better than a bad tax. ROBERT WAGNER

A moneylender serves you in the present tense, lends you in the conditional mood, keeps you in the subjunctive, and ruins you in the future.
JOSEPH ADDISON

Don't worry if you borrow, but worry if you lend. RUSSIAN PROVERB

If you would like to know the value of money, go and try to borrow some.
BENJAMIN FRANKLIN

"Whattaya got for collateral?"
"Whattaya need?"
"How about an eye?" SAM GIANCANA

The old woman who triumphantly announced that she had borrowed money enough to pay all her debts. P. L. LORD

The man who won't lend money isn't going to have many friends—or need them. WILSON MIZNER

Before borrowing money from a friend, decide which you need more.
ADDISON H. HALLOCK

If you have had enough of your friend, lend him some money.
RUSSIAN PROVERB

The human species, according to the best theory I can form of it, is composed of two distant races, the men who borrow, and the men who lend.
CHARLES LAMB

Don't borrow or lend, but if you must do one, lend. JOSH BILLINGS

The lender asks you to see him at your earliest convenience. ANON

We call our rich relatives the kin we love to touch. EDDIE CANTOR

It is better to borrow from a pessimist, as he never expects it back.
ANON

Lending money to a man makes him lose his memory.
FRENCH PROVERB

Loan-company officer to customer: "Gee, I'm sorry, Mr. Lenhart. I didn't realize we were talking so long—your first payment is due."
HOEST

They hired the money, didn't they? CALVIN COOLIDGE

Don't borrow from a nouveau riche. MALAY PROVERB

Great spenders are bad lenders. EDMUND FULLER

I know of nothing which gives a man a greater feeling of well-being than when he has touched a fellow for a tenner and got away with it.
EDGAR WALLACE

When I lend I am a friend; when I ask I am a foe.
SIXTEENTH-CENTURY PROVERB

A poor relation is the most irrelevant thing in nature.
CHARLES LAMB

If I had the privilege of making the Eleventh Commandment it would be this—Owe no man. JOSH BILLINGS

An old loan repaid is like finding something new.
RUSSIAN PROVERB

Acquaintance, n: a person whom we know well enough to borrow from, but not well enough to lend to. AMBROSE BIERCE

If you lend, you either lose the money or gain an enemy.
ALBANIAN PROVERB

You can't force anyone to love you or to lend you money.
JEWISH PROVERB

God bless pawnbrokers!
They are quiet men. MARGUERITE WILKINSON

A borrowed cloak does not keep you warm. ARABIAN PROVERB

If you lend money, you make a secret enemy; if you refuse it, an open one FRANCOIS VOLTAIRE

People may live as much retired from the world as they please; but sooner or later before they are aware, they will find themselves debtors or creditors to somebody. JOHANN WOLFGANG von GOETHE

In a narrow pass there is no borrower and no friend. ARAB PROVERB

Here lies old thirty-three-and-a-third percent
The more he got the more he lent,
The more he lent the more he craved—
Good Lord, can such a man be saved? ANON

Very often he that his money lends
Loses both his gold and his friends. CHARLES HADDON SPURGEON

Borrowers are nearly always ill-spenders, and it is with lent money that all evil is mainly done. JOHN RUSKIN

We are all of us richer than we think we are; but we are taught to borrow and to beg, and brought up more to make use of what is another's than of our own. MICHEL de MONTAIGNE

I can get no remedy against this consumption of the purse; borrowing only lingers and lingers it out, but the disease is incurable.
WILLIAM SHAKESPEARE

Accounting

When accounting,
Don't be rash;
There's no such thing
As "petty cash."

Net—the biggest word in the language of business.
HERBERT CASSON

When you make the mistake of adding the date to the right side of the accounting statement, you must add it to the left side too.
ACCOUNTANTS' MAXIM

Few have heard of Fra Luca Parioli, the inventor of double-entry bookkeeping; but he has probably had much more influence on human life than has Dante or Michelangelo. HERBERT J. MULLER

Our Accounting Department is the office that has the little red box on the wall saying "In case of emergency break glass." And inside are two tickets to Brazil. ROBERT ORBEN

A budget is telling your money where to go instead of wondering where it went. C. E. HOOVER

Auditors Are the People Who Go in After the War is Lost and Bayonet the Wounded. P. RUBIN

"Absorption of Overhead" is one of the most obscene terms I have ever heard. PETER F. DRUCKER

An accountant is a man hired to explain that you didn't make the money you thought you had. ANON

If my business was legitimate, I would deduct a substantial percentage for depreciation of my body. XAVIERA HOLLANDER

Budgeting is a system of additions and subtractions more honored in breach than in observance. EUGENE E. BRUSSELL

I don't know how much money I've got. I did ask the accountant how much it came to. I wrote it down on a bit of paper but I've lost the bit of paper. JOHN LENNON

Did you ever hear of a kid playing accountant—even if he wanted to be one? JACKIE MASON

Is Chapter Eleven the result of following the Ten Commandments? ANON

A budget tells us what we can't afford, but it doesn't keep us from buying it. WILLIAM FEATHER

Bankruptcy is a legal proceeding in which you put your money in your pants pocket and give your coat to your creditors. JOEY ADAMS

A budget is a method of worrying before you spend instead of afterwards. ANON

The law of diminishing returns holds good in almost every part of our human universe. ALDOUS LEONARD HUXLEY

Accounts receivable are bill-gotten gains. ROBERT ORBEN

There can be mathematicians of the first order who cannot count. BARON NOVALIS

Remember that even though work stops, nevertheless the expenses continue to mount up. MARCUS CATO

Budget: A mathematical confirmation of your suspicions. JOHN A. LINCOLN

A financial analyst thinks he sees the forest clearing but keeps bumping into the trees. EVAN ESAR

Evolution has her own accounting system and that's the only one that matters. R. BUCKMINISTER FULLER

A receiver is appointed by the court to take what's left. ROBERT FROST

Over the long haul of life on this planet, it is the ecologists, and not the bookkeepers of business, who are the ultimate accountants.
STEWART L. UDALL

It's simply a matter of creative accounting. MEL BROOKS

Those who work out our federal budget
Have a policy—really a honey—
We shall live on our national income,
Even if we must borrow the money! LEVERETT LYON

A budget is the way to go broke methodically. ANON

The loss which is unknown is no loss at all. PUBLILIUS SYRUS

Economy

Economy from us is good,
We take it without flinching.
From someone else it's understood
As downright penny-pinching.

He who will not economize will have to agonize. CONFUCIUS

It is not what we take up but what we give up that makes us rich.
HARRIET WARD BEECHER

Economy is going without something you do want in case you should, some day, want something which you probably won't want.
ANTHONY HOPE HAWKINS

Everybody is always in favour of general economy and particular expenditure. SIR ANTHONY EDEN

Economy is denying yourself a necessity today in order to buy a luxury tomorrow. ANON

False economy is not spending money on a sunny day because you're saving it for a rainy day. EVAN ESAR

Persons who have never made or saved a dollar are always telling me how to spend a million. HENRY FORD

A budget is what you stay within if you go without.
CLAUDE McDONALD

The best way to reduce your bills is to put them on microfilm. ANON

While other corporations economize on pencils and paper clips, the *Times* saves money on chairs. WILL WENG

Economy is cutting down other people's wages. J. B. MORTON

The richest man is the most economical. The poorest man is the miser.
SEBASTIAN ROCH NICHOLAS CHAMFORT

I would rather have my people laugh at my economies than weep for my extravagance. OSCAR II of SWEDEN

He practiced the utmost economy in order to keep up the most expensive habits. GEORGE BERNARD SHAW

Take care of the pence, and the pounds will take care of themselves.
WILLIAM LOWNDES

Beware of little expenses; a small leak will sink a great ship.
BENJAMIN FRANKLIN

Some say you shouldn't prune except at the right time of the year. I generally do it when the saw is sharp. GEORGE AIKEN

A sharp knife cuts the quickest and hurts the least.
KATHARINE HEPBURN

Take care to be an economist in prosperity; there is no fear of your being one in adversity. JOHANN GEORG ZIMMERMANN

Economy is the art of making the most of life. The love of economy is the root of all virtue. GEORGE BERNARD SHAW

Teach thrift to all with whom you come in contact; you never know when you may need their savings to finance one of your ventures.
DONALD ROBERT PERRY MARQUIS

Economy: the wealth of the poor and the wisdom of the rich.
ALEXANDRE DUMAS

Men do not realize how great a revenue economy is.
MARCUS TULLIUS CICERO

Without economy none can be rich, and with it few can be poor.
SAMUEL JOHNSON

Expense, and great expense, may be an essential part of true economy.
EDMUND BURKE

I favor the policy of economy, not because I wish to save money, but because I wish to save people. CALVIN COOLIDGE

Economy is too late at the bottom of the purse.
LUCIUS ANNAEUS SENECA

Economy is half the battle of life; it is not so hard to earn money as to spend it well. CHARLES HADDON SPURGEON

Economy is a distributive virtue, and consists not in saving but in selection. EDMUND BURKE

Economy before competence is meanness after it; therefore, economy is for the poor: the rich may dispense with it.
CHRISTIAN NESTELL BOVEE

Be not penny-wise; riches have wings, and sometimes they fly away of themselves; sometimes they must be set flying to bring in more.
FRANCIS BACON

I am a strict economist; not, indeed, for the sake of the money; but one of the principal parts in my composition is a kind of pride of stomach; and I scorn to fear the face of any man living. ROBERT BURNS

After order and liberty, economy is one of the highest essentials of a free government . . . Economy is always a guarantee of peace.
CALVIN COOLIDGE

V BACKGROUND

Economics

Give the minimum,
Gain the maximum.

I learned more about economics from one South Dakota dust storm than I did in all my years in college. HUBERT HUMPHREY

The trouble with today's economy is that when a man is rich, it's all on paper. When he's broke, it's cash. SAM MARCONI

One of the greatest pieces of economic wisdom is to know what you do not know. JOHN KENNETH GALBRAITH

A completely planned economy ensures that when no bacon is delivered, no eggs are delivered at the same time. LEO FRAIN

It's called political economy because it has nothing to do with either politics or economy. STEPHEN LEACOCK

Political economy: two words that should be divorced—on Grounds of Incompatability. *The Wall Street Journal*

Our nation's economy seems to be based on the belief that we shouldn't practice it. HAROLD COFFIN

In economics, the majority is always wrong. ANON

One of the difficulties of economics is that it is too easy to explain after a particular event has happened, why it should have happened; and too easy to explain before it happens, why it should not happen.

M. G. KENDALL

A study of economics usually reveals that the best time to buy anything is last year. MARTY ALLEN

To have national prosperity we need to spend, but to have individual prosperity we must save. ANON

The economy may suffer if auto sales drop—but that's the American way; we have to buy more cars than we need or we'll never be able to afford them. JACK WILSON

If ignorance paid dividends, most Americans could make a fortune out of what they don't know about economics. LUTHER HODGES

Everything now seems to be under federal control except the national debt and the budget. BOB GODDARD

There are three things not worth running for—a bus, a woman or a new economic panacea: if you wait a bit another will come along.

DERICK HEATHCOAT AMORY

The American economy is the eighth wonder of the world, and the ninth is the economic ignorance of the American people. BURTON CRANE

There's one way to solve all the econommic problems of the country. Make complacency taxable. ANON

Economics is all about the two biggest problems of life: how to make money and how to get along without it. ANON

We have become to some extent, I think, economic hypochondriacs. You get a wiggle in a statistic . . . and everyone runs to get the thermometer. PAUL W. McCRACKEN

What is wholly mysterious in economics is not likely to be important.

JOHN KENNETH GALBRAITH

Economics is like being lost in the woods. How can you tell where you are going when you don't even know where you are? ANON

What economic history needs at present is not more documents but a pair of stout boots.
R. H. TAWNEY

Economics is a subject that does not greatly respect one's wishes.
NIKITA KHRUSHCHEV

One of the soundest rules I try to remember when making forecasts in the field of economics is that whatever is to happen is happening already.
SYLVIA PORTER

Nine out of ten economic laws are economic laws only till they are found out.
ROBERT LYND

Modern political theory seems to hold that the way to keep the economy in the pink is to run the government in the red.
NATHAN NIELSEN

A systematic application and critical evaluation of the basic analytic concepts of economic theory, with an emphasis on money and why it's good. Fixed coefficient production functions, cost and supply curves, and nonconvexity comprise the first semester, with the second semester concentrating on spending, making change, and keeping a neat wallet. The Federal Reserve System is analyzed, and advanced students are coached in the proper method of filling out a deposit slip. Other topics include inflation and depression—how to dress for each—loans interest, welching.
WOODY ALLEN

The idea of imposing restrictions on a free economy to assure freedom of competition is like breaking a man's leg to make him run faster.
N. R. SAYRE

An economic system prouder of the distribution of its products than of the products themselves.
MURRAY KEMPTON

Economics is about the cost of our appetites.
GEORGE F. WILL

A nation is not in danger of financial disaster merely because it owes itself money.
ANDREW WILLIAM MELLON

Like theology, and unlike mathematics, economics deals with matters which men consider very close to their lives.
JOHN KENNETH GALBRAITH

The only type of economic structure in which government is free and in which the human spirit is free is one in which commerce is free.
THOMAS ARNOLD

There are in the field of economic events no constant relations, and consequently no measurement is possible. LUDWIG ELDER von MISES

The most important law in the whole of political economy is the law of "variety" in human wants; each separate want is soon satisfied, and yet there is no end to wants. W. S. JEVONS

We may go down in history as an elegant technological society which underwent biological disintegration through lack of economic understanding. DAVID M. GATES

The dynamo of our economic system is self-interest which may range from mere petty greed to admirable types of self-expression.
FELIX FRANKFURTER

Economists

All economists deal in fiction
And I think it's rather funny,
That few of them back their prediction
With one little bit of their money.

An economist is an expert who will know tomorrow why the things he predicted yesterday didn't happen today. LAURENCE J. PETER

A man accustomed to think in millions—other people's millions.
ARNOLD BENNETT

Practical men who believe themselves exempt from any intellectual influence, are usually the slaves of some defunct economist.
JOHN MAYNARD KEYNES

Don't put the fate of your business in the delusion of economists.
PETER F. DRUCKER

Once economists were asked, "If you're so smart, why ain't you rich?" Today they're asked, "Now you've proved you ain't so smart, how come you got so rich?" EDGAR R. FIEDLER

The economists who are most highly regarded in their own time have almost always been those who confined themselves to abstract speculation unmarred by social purpose. JOHN KENNETH GALBRAITH

Economics is too important to be left to economists. LOUIS STONE

An economist is a man who states the the obvious in terms of the incomprehensible. ALFRED A. KNOPF

I have been gradually coming under the conviction, disturbing for a professional theorist, that there is no such thing as economics.
KENNETH E. BOULDING

A person who knows all about money but has none.
J. MARVIN PETERSON

To me, economics is a kind of sad profession, although it is the one profession where you can gain great eminence without ever being right.
GEORGE MEANY

An economist is a man who knows how to throw the money he hasn't got after the money he never had. EVAN ESAR

Economics is an extremely useful form of employment for economists.
ANON

Can't someone bring me a one-handed economist?
HARRY S. TRUMAN

Economists are almost invariably engaged in defeating the last slump.
STUART CHASE

If economists could manage to get themselves thought of as humble, competent people, like dentists, that would be splendid.
JOHN MAYNARD KEYNES

If the nation's economists were laid end to end, they would still point in all directions. ARTHUR H. MOTLEY

If all economists were laid end to end, they would not reach a conclusion.
GEORGE BERNARD SHAW

In all recorded history there has not been one economist who has had to worry about where the next meal would come from.
PETER F. DRUCKER

The economy depends about as much on economists as the weather does on weather forecasters.
JEAN-PAUL KAUFFMAN

Madmen in authority, who hear voices in the air, are distilling their frenzy from some academic scribbler of a few years back.
JOHN MAYNARD KEYNES

Economists are economical, among other things, of ideas. They make those they acquire as graduate students do for a lifetime. Changes in economics come only with changing generations.
JOHN KENNETH GALBRAITH

Economists now say we move in cycles instead of running around in circles. It sounds better, but it means the same.
ANON

The instability of the economy is equaled only by the instability of economists.
PROFESSOR JOHN H. WILLIAMS

There's nothing an economist should fear so much as applause.
HERBERT MARSHALL

Economists will tell you how to get a better standard of living, but not how to keep up with it.
ANON

It is a commonplace among thinking economists that a dollar bill will go just so far and no farther at a given time and place, the same law of nature holding true for bills of other denominations, such as $2 bills, $5 bills, and so on, and even truer for the more familiar nickel, dime and quarter.
WILL CUPPY

The ideas of economists and political philosophers, both when they are right and when they are wrong, are more powerful than is commonly understood. Indeed, the world is ruled by little else.
JOHN MAYNARD KEYNES

There are men regarded today as brilliant economists, who deprecate saving and recommend squandering on a national scale as the way of economic salvation; and when anyone points to what the consequences of these policies will be in the long run, they reply flippantly, as might the prodigal son of a warning father: "In the long run we are all dead."
HENRY HAZLITT

Capitalism

Capitalism is when
It sees Communism worse.
One is men exploiting men,
The other quite the reverse.

The American system of ours, call it Americanism, call it Capitalism, call it what you like, gives each and every one of us a great opportunity if we only seize it with both hands and make the most of it. AL CAPONE

Until you understand Capitalism you do not understand human society as it exists at present. GEORGE BERNARD SHAW

Capitalism equals love of money in my view, and we didn't start out that way. We started out with a love of individual enterprise.
ERIC SLOANE

Capitalism is like this: Forty years ago lead was added to gasoline and the price went up. Now lead is being removed from gasoline and the price went up. ROBERT ORBEN

Capitalism is based on private property, where normal economic activity consists of commercial transactions between consenting adults.
IRVING KRISTOL

The leaders of the French Revolution excited the poor against the rich; this made the rich poor, but it never made the poor rich.
FISHER AMES

I think that Capitalism, wisely managed, can probably be made more efficient for attaining economic ends than any alternative system yet in sight, but that in itself it is in many ways extremely objectionable.
JOHN MAYNARD KEYNES

Capitalist production begets, with the inexorability of a law of nature, its own negation. KARL MARX

American capitalism has been both overpraised and overindicted; it is neither the Plumed Knight nor the monstrous Robber Baron.
MAX LERNER

Democratic capitalism, combined with industrial democracy, is unquestionably the best way of life for mankind. DAVID J. McDONALD

The public be damned! I'm working for my stockholders.
WILLIAM HENRY VANDERBILT

The weapon of capital is potentially one of the most powerful and least used in the Western world. Poland affords us a chance to use it. It might turn out to be our only effective way, in the long run, of bringing about change behind the Iron Curtain. FELIX ROBATYA

Another thing about capitalism—everybody knows who's in Grant's tomb. LOUIS NELSON BOWMAN

When labor quarrels with capital, or capital neglects the interests of labor, it is like the hand thinking it does not need the eye, the ear or the brain. JAMES FREEMAN CLARKE

The dynamics of capitalism is postponement of enjoyment to the constantly postponed future. NORMAN O. BROWN

In the progress of time, and through our own base carelessness and ignorance, we have permitted the money industry, by the virtue of its business, to gradually attain a political and economic influence so powerful that it has actually undermined the authority of the state and usurped the power of democratic government. VINCENT C. VICKERS

Pappenbacker says that every time you are polite to a proletarian you are helping to bolster up the capitalist system. EVELYN WAUGH

The forces of a capitalist society, if left unchecked, tend to make the rich richer and the poor poorer. JAWAHARIAL NEHRU

These capitalists generally act harmoniously and in concert to fleece the public. ABRAHAM LINCOLN

We must especially beware of that small group of selfish men who would clip the wings of the American eagle in order to feather their own nests. FRANKLIN DELANO ROOSEVELT

I spent 33 years (in the Marines) . . . being a high-class muscleman for big business, for Wall Street and the bankers. On shore, I was a racketeer for capitalism. . . . I helped purify Nicaragua for the international banking house of Brown Brothers. . . . I helped make Mexico . . . safe for Americal oil interests. . . . I brought light to the Dominican Republic for American sugar interests. . . . I helped Make Haiti and Cuba decent places for National City Bank boys to collect revenue. . . . I helped in the rape of half a dozen Central American republics for the benefit of Wall Street. In China . . . I helped see to it that Standard Oil went its way. . . . I might have given Al Capone a few hints.
SMEDLEY BUTLER

There is in the capitalist system a tendency towards self-destruction.
ANON

Capitalism has destroyed our belief in any effective power but that of self-interest backed by force. GEORGE BERNARD SHAW

The word is CAPITALISM. We are too mealymouthed. We fear the word CAPITALISM is unpopular. So we talk about the "free enterprise system" and run to cover in the folds of the flag and talk about the American Way of Life. ERIC ALLEN JOHNSTON

Each needs the other: capital cannot do without labor, nor labor without capital. POPE LEO XIII

Capitalism in the United States has undergone profound modification, not just under the New Deal but through a consensus that continued to grow after the New Deal. Government in the U.S. today is a senior partner in every business in the country. NORMAN COUSINS

Capital is a result of labor, and is used by labor to assist it in further production. Labor is the active and initial force, and labor is therefore the employer of capital. HENRY GEORGE

What we mean when we say we are for or against capitalism is that we like or dislike a certain civilization or scheme of life.
J. A. SCHUMPETER

History suggests that capitalism is a necessary condition for British freedom. Clearly, it is not a sufficient condition. MILTON FRIEDMAN

The capitalist process, not by coincidence but by virtue of its mechanism, progressively raises the standards of life of the masses. It does so through a sequence of vicissitudes, the severity of which is proportional to the speed of the advance. JOSEPH ALOIS SCHUMPETER

Anti-Capitalism

When you've not
Got a lot,
The getter
Is better
Just to share
Doctrinaire
With the theft
Of the left.

The Communist party is the biggest corporation of all. JOHN DOS PASSOS

Communists are frustrated Capitalists. ERIC HOFFER

Marxist Law of the Distribution of Wealth: Shortages will be divided equally among the peasants. JOHN GUSTAFSON

Communism is like prohibition, it's a good idea but it won't work. WILL ROGERS

As with the Christian religion, the worst advertisement for Socialism is its adherents. GEORGE ORWELL

Lewis always wrote his name john l. lewis, so strong was he against capital. GERALD F. LIEBERMAN

Industrial crisis, unemployment, waste, widespread poverty, these are the incurable diseases of capitalism. JOSEPH STALIN

Under capitalism we have a state in the proper sense of the word; that is, a special machine for the suppression of one class by another.
NIKOLAI LENIN

Communism is idiocy. They want to divide up the property. Suppose they did it. It requires brains to keep money as well as to make it. In a precious little while the money would be back in the former owner's hands and the communist would be poor again. The division would have to be remade every three years or it would do the communist no good.
MARK TWAIN

By no stretch of the imagination would Jesus have been a socialist.
The REVEREND NORMAN VINCENT PEALE

A Communist is one who has yearnings
For equal division of unequal earnings.
EBENEZER ELLIOTT

If capital and labor ever do get together it's good-night for the rest of us.
ABE MARTIN

You show me a capitalist, I'll show you a bloodsucker. MALCOLM X

There is no more demoralizing theory than that which imputes all human evils to Capitalism or any other single agency. SAMUEL GOMPERS

The capitalists will sell us the length of rope with which we will destroy them. NIKOLAI LENIN

Communism is based on the belief that man is so weak and inadequate that he is unable to govern himself, and therefore requires the rule of strong masters. HARRY S. TRUMAN

Capital and labor should be one—but which one? EVAN ESAR

If you divorce capital from labor, capital is hoarded, and labor starves.
DANIEL WEBSTER

The inherent vice of capitalism is the unequal sharing of blessings; the inherent virtue of socialism is the equal sharing of miseries.
WINSTON CHURCHILL

"The trouble with socialism," a European observer once remarked, 'is socialism. The trouble with capitalism is capitalists."
WILLIAM F. BUCKLEY

The crippling of individuals I consider the worst evil of capitalism. Our whole educational system suffers from this evil. An exaggerated competitive attitude is inculcated into the student, who is trained to worship acquisitive success as a preparation for his future career.

ALBERT EINSTEIN

The fear of capitalism has compelled socialism to widen freedom and the fear of socialism has compelled capitalism to increase equality.

WILL & ARIEL DURANT

The word Capitalism is misleading. The proper name for our system is Proletarianism. GEORGE BERNARD SHAW

You talk about capitalism and communism and all that sort of thing, but the important thing is the struggle everybody is engaged in to get better living conditions, and they are not interested too much in the form of government. BERNARD BARUCH

Capitalism inevitably and by virtue of the very logic of its civilization creates, educates and subsidizes a vested interest in social unrest.

JOSEPH ALOIS SCHUMPTER

No society can surely be flourishing and happy of which the far greater part of the members are poor and miserable. ADAM SMITH

Communism is a hateful thing and a menace to peace and organized government; but the communism of combined wealth and capital, the outgrowth of overweening cupidity and selfishness, which insideously undermines the justice and integrity of free institutions, is not less dangerous than the communism of oppressed poverty and toil, which, exasperated by injustice and discontent, attacks with wild disorder the citadel of rule. GROVER CLEVELAND

Free Enterprise

When enterprise is named as free,
In spite of that there is a fee;
It means you can do what you will,
It doesn't mean there is no bill.

A salesman is the foot soldier of free enterprise. ANON

Private enterprise makes O.K. private action which would be considered dishonest in public action. JOHN F. KENNEDY

In business the man who engages in the most adventures is surest to come out unhurt. EDMUND FULLER

The private enterprise system really consists of harnessing men, money and ideas, and the genius of inventors and technologists with the savings of the thousands. MALCOLM MUIR

Nobody talks more of free enterprise and competition and of the best man winning than the man who inherited his father's store or farm.
C. WRIGHT MILLS

Essential to a system of free enterprise is a climate in which new, small and independent business can be conceived and born, can grow and prosper. WILLIAM B. BENTON

The business world worships mediocrity. Officially, we revere free enterprise, initiative and individuality. Unofficially we fear it.
GEORGE LOIS

Extinguish free enterprise and you extinguish liberty.
MARGARET THATCHER

Some people regard private enterprise as a predatory tiger to be shot. Others look on it as a cow they can milk. Not enough people see it as a healthy horse pulling a sturdy wagon. SIR WINSTON CHURCHILL

Private enterprise is ceasing to be free enterprise.
FRANKLIN DELANO ROOSEVELT

Once you prime the pump of free enterprise, it doesn't stop where you want it. STANLEY K. HATHAWAY

We stand for the maintenance of private property . . . we shall protect free enterprise as the most expedient, or rather the sole possible economic order. ADOLF HITLER

The very survival of free enterprise depends upon a rising standard of living and an expanding economy. HARRY S. TRUMAN

The free enterprise system is a way of economic life, open to hope—an economy open to new ideas, new products, new jobs, new men.
WILLIAM B. BENTON

The secret of free enterprise is that we harness the natural instincts of each man to serve himself, and rely on other natural forces to see that as he serves himself he serves society. CLARENCE B. RANDALL

Private enterprise, indeed, became too private. It became privileged enterprise, not free enterprise. FRANKLIN DELANO ROOSEVELT

If a free society cannot help the many who are poor, it cannot save the few who are rich. JOHN F. KENNEDY

With all the mass media concentrated in a few hands, the ancient faith in the competition of ideas in the free market seems like a hollow echo of a much simpler day. KINGMAN BREWSTER

If we in business cannot put the brakes on this creeping socialism, the free enterprise system will become a thing of the past.
BARTON A. CUMMINGS

Private capital and private management are entitled to adequate reward for efficiency, but business must recognize that its reward results from the employment of the resources of the nation. HARRY S. TRUMAN

We need a free economy not only for the renewed material prosperity it will bring, but because it is indispensable to individual freedom, human dignity and to a more just, more honest society.
MARGARET THATCHER

What good does it do the world for the governments to sit down at peace tables and to work out the fine political mechanisms if they leave the instruments of economic and technical power in the hands of unrestrained private individuals and corporations?
HARLEY M. KILGORE

Ours is a program whose basic thesis is not that the system of free private enterprise has failed . . . but that it has not yet been tried.
FRANKLIN DELANO ROOSEVELT

Free enterprise: A huge area of the American economy that is still noticeable to observe with peripheral vision after they subtract the public sector, conglomerates, federally supported agriculture, monopolies, duopolies, and oligopolies. BERNARD ROSENBERG

In private enterprises men may advance or recede, whereas they who aim at empire have no alternative between the highest success and utter downfall. CORNELIUS TACITUS

Of course I believe in free enterprise, but in my system of free enterprise, the democratic principle is that there never was, never has been, never will be room for the ruthless exploitation of the many for the benefit of the few. HARRY S. TRUMAN

Beware of that profound enemy of the free enterprise system who pays lip service to free competition—but also labels every anti-trust prosecution as a "persecution." FRANKLIN DELANO ROOSEVELT

Figures

I can never tell why
They say figures don't lie;
Just look at the mystics,
Who cook up statistics.

It does not follow that because something can be counted it therefore should be counted. HAROLD L. ENARSON

Round numbers are always false. SAMUEL JOHNSON

Every true American likes to think in terms of thousands and millions The world "million" is probably the most pleasure-giving vocable in the language. AGNES REPPLIER

Has it never occurred to you that the Romans counted backwards?
WALTER C. SELLAR & ROBERT J. YEATMAN

Some customers say that number three is the magic number and some say number seven. It's neither, my friend, neither. It's number one.
CHARLES DICKENS

There is no safety in numbers, or in anything else. JAMES THURBER

Women have a passion for mathematics. They divide their ages by two, double the price of their dresses, trebel their husband's salaries and add five years to the ages of their best friends. MARCEL ACHARD

Three men were asked to add two and two The first man answered thirty six, the second man answered Wednesday and finally the third said four. When asked to explain how he got this correct, he said, Simple. I just took thirty-six from Wednesday. ANON

We used to think that if we knew one, we knew two, because one and one are two We are finding that we must learn a great deal more about "and."
SIR ARTHUR EDDINGTON

Mediocrity adds two and two, and gets only four. HENRY S. HASKINS

The formula "Two and Two make Five" is not without its attractions.
FYODOR MIKHAILOVICH DOSTOEVSKY

There is a difference between a psychopath and a neurotic. A psychopath thinks two and two are five. A neurotic knows that two and two are four, but he worries about it. ANON

What men usually ask of God when they pray is that two and two not make four. ANON

I've seen farmers who can't read and farmers who can't write, but I've never seen a farmer who can't figure. FORREST HILL

To think that two and two are four
And neither five nor three
The heart of man has long been sore
And long 'tis like to be. ALFRED EDWARD HOUSMAN

Two and two continue to make four, in spite of the whine of the amateur for three, or the cry of the critic for five.
JAMES ABBOT McNEIL WHISTLER

It would take nearly 10,000 years to count up to one billion.

It is the nature of all greatness not to be exact. EDMUND BURKE

My sympathy often goes out for the humble decimal point. He has a pathetic and hectic life wandering around among regimental ciphers, trying to find some of the old places he used to know when budgets were balanced HERBERT HOOVER

Who can really feel comfortable in this culture now except maybe a few guys who are good at mathematics? THOMAS HART BENTON

It has been said that figures rule the world; maybe. I am quite sure that it is figures which show us whether it is being ruled well or badly. JOHANN WOLFGANG von GOETHE

A few honest men are better than numbers. OLIVER CROMWELL

That is like assuring the non-swimmer that he can safely walk across a river because its average depth is only four feet. MILTON FRIEDMAN

A politician who can't feel a situation without having diagrams drawn up for him is no kind of politician. LYNDON BAINES JOHNSON

It is told that such are the aerodynamics and wing-loading of the bumblebee that, in principle, it cannot fly If this be true, life among bumblebees must bear a remarkable resemblance to life in the United States. JOHN KENNETH GALBRAITH

As far as the laws of mathematics refer to reality, they are not certain, and as far as they are certain, they do not refer to reality. ALBERT EINSTEIN

Oh, don't tell me of facts—I never believe facts: you know Canning said nothing was so fallacious as facts, except figures. SYDNEY SMITH

Facts and figures illustrating [economic] progress fly across frontiers like guided missiles directed at people's minds. And, of course, those who lag behind in such progress are the most exposed to this propaganda. PIERRE MENDES-FRANCE

Banking

At the bank there's no disguising
And never long before it's known:
He who writes the advertising
Is not the man who makes the loan.

I've always found that a gambler's word is better than a banker's AL FARB

Banking may well be a career from which no man really recovers.
JOHN GALBRAITH

I go to the bank every morning and when I say "No," I return home at night without worry But when I say "Yes" it's like putting your finger into a machine—the whirring wheels may drag your whole body in after the finger.
SIR NATHAN MEYER ROTHSCHILD

There is a certain Buddhistic calm that comes from having . . . money in the bank.
TOM ROBBINS

When a poor man has too much money, he lends it to the bank; when a rich man hasn't enough, the bank lends it to him.
ANON

Five banks a year on the average are shut down because of embezzlements.
L. M. BOYD

Women are like banks, boy. Breaking and entering is a serious business.
JOE ORTON

A banker without money is like a doctor without pills.
GEORGE WOODS

Most banks will gladly grant a loan.
In fact, they often speed it;
The only thing that they require
Is proof that you don't need it.
F. G. KERNAN

If money doesn't grow on trees, why do banks have so many branches?
LEOPOLD FECHTNER

Long ago, the Englishman's castle was his home; then, that went, and his home became his castle. Now his castle is the nation's and his home is the bank's.
LEON GARFIELD

A bank is the thing that will always lend you money if you can prove that you don't need it
JOE E. LEWIS

We don't issue loans to writers, artists and tap dancers.
NEW YORK BANKER

It is a rather pleasant experience to be alone in a bank at night.
WILLIE SUTTON

If it's so easy to borrow money from a bank, why should anyone want to rob it? ANON

I cried all the way to the bank. LIBERACE

A bank is a place where they lend you an umbrella in fair weather and ask for it back again when it begins to rain. ROBERT FROST

My brother down in Texas
Can't even write his name
He signs his cheques with Xs
But they cash 'em just the same. IRVING BERLIN

When a draft passes through a bank, does it give the clerk a cold? LEOPOLD FECHTNER

Soon banks will have special windows for hold-ups. ANON

Banking establishments are more dangerous than standing armies. THOMAS JEFFERSON

A bank's resources should be handled as a general handles his soldiers—you should be strong in reserves. You must be ready to send reinforcements wherever needed. You must send your soldier-dollars wherever they can do the most good. JAMES STILLMAN

I can hold a note as long as the Chase National Bank. ETHEL MERMAN

Among the books with unhappy endings are checkbooks. ANON

Is your husband losing interest? He won't if he banks with us. ANON

Why can't some yes-men be bank cashiers? HERBERT V. PROCHNOW

Our banking system grew up by accident; and whenever something happens by accident, it becomes a religion WALTER B. WRISTON

Foundations of a new religion can be laid only with the blessing of the bankers SALVADOR DALI

Verily what bishops are to the English, bankers are to Americans. MABEL ULRICH

There has probably very rarely ever been so happy a position as that of a London private banker: and never perhaps a happier.
WALTER BAGEHOT

When you want really big money, you usually find yourself talking to people who didn't go to Eton. AN ENGLISH BANKER

A sound banker, alas, is not one who sees danger and avoids it, but one who, when he is ruined, is ruined in a conventional and orthodox way along with his fellows, so that no one can really blame him.
JOHN MAYNARD KEYNES

I don't believe in principle,
But oh, I do in interest. JAMES R. LOWELL

The introduction of a bank . . . has a powerful tendency to extend the active capital of a country. It is probable that they will be established wherever they can exist with advantage and wherever they can be supported. If administered with prudence they will add new energies to all pecuniary operations. ALEXANDER HAMILTON

Tax

After Government subtraction
From the sum that we inject,
Our benefit's a fraction
Of what we should collect.

Our forefathers made one mistake. What they should have fought for was representation without taxation. FLETCHER KNEBEL

Why does a slight tax increase cost you $200 and a substantial tax cut save you 30 cents? PEG BRACKEN

The hardest thing in the world to understand is the income tax.
ALBERT EINSTEIN

The Eiffel Tower is the Empire State Building after taxes. ANON

The taxpayer—that's someone who works for the federal government but doesn't have to take a civil service examination. RONALD REAGAN

Next to being shot at and missed, nothing is quite as satisfying as an income tax refund. F. J. RAYMOND

Tax is the fine we pay for thriving. ANON

Alexander Hamilton originated the put and take system in our national treasury; the taxpayers put it in and the politicians take it out. WILL ROGERS

Charitable donations can be deducted from income tax. But they must also be deducted from income. ANON

Folly taxes us four times as much as Congress. ANON

I wanted my son to share in the business but the government beat him to it. *Reader's Digest*

I'm proud to be paying taxes in the United States. The only thing is—I could be just as proud for half the money. ARTHUR GODFREY

There's only one thing worse than paying income tax; and that's not paying it! ANON

The rich aren't like us, they pay less taxes PETER DE VRIES

Taxes are going up so fast that government is likely to price itself right out of the market. DAN BENNETT

Taxation is the process by which money is collected from the people to pay the salaries of those who do the collecting. ANON

Tax reform means, "Don't tax you, don't tax me. Tax that fellow behind the tree." RUSSELL LONG

A democracy allows complete control over how we pay our taxes—cash, check or money order. ANON

Never sell America short. In what other country can a boy start with nothing and wind up with enough after taxes to give him a fresh start? FLETCHER KNEBEL

Ah, for those good old days when Uncle Sam lived within his income—and without most of yours. BARCLAY BRADEN

On door of a tax office: "Sorry, we're open." ROD BROWNING

The income tax has made more liars out of the American people than golf has. Even when you make a tax form out on the level, you don't know when it's through if you are a crook or a martyr. WILL ROGERS

Always overpay your income taxes That way, you'll get a refund.
MEYER LANSKY

There is one difference between a tax collector and a taxidermist; the taxidermist leaves the hide. MORTIMER J. CAPLIN

A minister of finance is a legally authorized pickpocket.
PAUL RAMADIER

All money nowadays seems to be produced with a natural homing instinct for the Treasury. PRINCE PHILIP

Positive thinking is when you work forty-eight hours a week in a steel mill: have a part time job as a janitor; drive a cab on weekends; and when you write out the check to pay your income tax, you say, "Easy come, Easy go!" ROBERT ORBEN

I consider it my patriotic duty to keep Elvis in the 90 percent tax bracket. COLONEL TOM PARKER

In levying taxes and in shearing sheep it is well to stop when you get down to the skin. AUSTIN O'MALLEY

If the Lord loveth a cheerful giver, how he must hate the taxpayer!
JOHN ANDREW HOLMES

Not only is it more blessed to give than receive—it is also deductible.
ANON

I have some money; not much since I paid my taxes
CHARLES M. SCHWAB

The point to remember is that what the government gives it must first take away. JOHN S. COLEMAN

Today, it takes more brains and effort to make out the income-tax form than it does to make the income. ALFRED E. NEUMAN

The reward of energy, enterprise and thrist—is taxes.
WILLIAM FEATHER

The art of taxation consists in so plucking the goose as to obtain the largest amount of feathers with the least amount of hissing.
JEAN BAPTISTE COLBERT

When an Englishman is totally incapable of doing any work whatsoever, he describes himself in the income-tax form as a "gentleman."
ROBERT LYND

When everybody has got money they cut taxes, and when they're broke they raise 'em. That's statesmanship of the highest order.
WILL ROGERS

My age is 39 plus tax. LIBERACE

To produce an income tax return that has any depth to it, any feeling, one must have lived—and suffered. FRANK SULLIVAN

In general, the art of government consists in making as much money as possible from our class of citizens to give to the other.
FRANCOIS VOLTAIRE

Capital punishment—The income tax. JEFF HAYES

A tax cut is the kindest cut of all. ANON

Of all debts, men are least willing to pay their taxes; what a satire this is on government. RALPH WALDO EMERSON

Taxes, after all, are the dues that we pay for the privileges of membership in an organized society. FRANKLIN DELANO ROOSEVELT

Taxation without representation is tyranny. JAMES OTIS

Protect the birds. The dove brings peace and the stork brings tax exemption. ANON

The wisdom of man never yet contrived a system of taxation that would operate with perfect equality. ANDREW JACKSON

Noah must have taken into the Ark two taxes, one male and one female, and did they multiply beautifully: Next to guinea pigs, taxes must have been the most prolific animals. WILL ROGERS

Governments last as long as the under-taxed can defend themselves against the over-taxed. BERNARD BERENSON

Anybody has a right to evade taxes if he can get away with it. No citizen has a moral obligation to assist in maintaining the government. If Congress insists on making stupid mistakes and passing foolish tax laws, millionaires should not be condemned if they take advantage of them.
J. P. MORGAN

We owe it to our country to pay our taxes without murmuring: the time to get in our fine work is on the valuation. EDGAR WILSON NYE

The apportionment of taxes on the various descriptions of property is an act which seems to require the most exact impartiality; yet there is, perhaps, no legislative act in which greater opportunity and temptation are given to a predominant party to trample on the rules of justice.
JAMES MADISON

Errors in taxation are visited on everybody. OTTO KUHN

Congress should know how to levy taxes, and if it doesn't know how to collect them, then a man is a fool to pay the taxes. J. P. MORGAN

History shows that when the taxes of a nation approach about 20 percent of the people's income, there begins to be a lack of respect for government. . . . When it reaches 25 percent, there comes an increase in lawlessness. RONALD REAGAN

An unlimited power to tax involves, necessarily, the power to destroy.
DAVID WEBSTER

To tax and to please, no more than to love and to be wise, is not given to men. EDMUND BURKE

Collecting more taxes than is absolutely necessary is legalized robbery.
CALVIN COOLIDGE

The higher taxes go, the sharper the voter grinds his ax. ANON

It is essential that you should practically bear in mind that toward the payment of debts here must be revenue; that to have revenue there must be taxes; that no taxes can be devised which are not more or less inconvenient and unpleasant; that the intrinsic embarrassment inseparable from the selection of the proper objects (which is always a choice of difficulties) ought to be a decisive motive for candid construction of the government in making it and for a spirit of acquiescence in the measures for obtaining revenue which the public exigencies may at any time dictate.
GEORGE WASHINGTON

The City

Oh! What a pity
The city's not pretty,
But that's where we go
To make all that dough.

New York is a little strip of an island with a row of well fed folks up and down the middle, and a lot of hungry folks on each side.
HARRY L. WILSON

I've heard it said that the American city lacks everything from which no profit is possible.
WILFRED OWEN

A town that has no ceiling price,
A town of double-talk;
A town so big men name her twice,
Like so: "N'Yawk, N'Yawk"
CHRISTOPHER MORLEY

A prison for speculative minds.
FRANZ MEHRING

The chicken is the country's, but the city eats it.
GEORGE HERBERT

The outcome of the cities will depend on the race between the automobile and the elevator, and anyone who bets on the elevator is crazy.
FRANK LLOYD WRIGHT

Public service is my motto.
AL CAPONE

A phenomenon growing so fast its arteries are showing through its outskirts.
CLYDE MOORE

I don't know what London's coming to—the higher the buildings the lower the morals.
NOEL COWARD

I love to go to Washington—if only to be near my money. BOB HOPE

If you stay in Beverly Hills too long you become a Mercedes.
ROBERT REDFORD

If a man can live in Manhattan, he can live anywhere.
ARTHUR C. CLARKE

Any city, however small, is in fact divided into two, one the city of the poor, the other of the rich; these are at war with one another. PLATO

One look at the rush-hour jam in the subway and you know why no one rides it any more.
JOHN CIARDI

New York is the city of right angles and tough, damaged people.
PETE HAMILL

Farmers worry only during the growing season, but town people worry all the time.
EDGAR WATSON HOWE

The city is not a concrete jungle. It is a human zoo.
DESMOND MORRIS

Washington, D.C., means Washington Demands Cash.
JACK HERBERT

The people are the city. WILLIAM SHAKESPEARE

Out in the country, life is what you make it, but in the city it too often is what you make.
ANON

Cities are full of people with whom a certain degree of contact is useful and enjoyable, but you do not want them in your hair. And they do not want you in theirs either.
JANE JACOBS

The word for New York is activity. V. S. PRITCHETT

If there were one city I should pick to live in, it would be New York. It is a city where I walk down the street and feel anything is possible.
MARIA SCHELL

Cities force growth and make men talkative and entertaining, but they make them artificial.
RALPH WALDO EMERSON

New York is a city where everyone mutinies but no one deserts.
HARRY HERSHFIELD

In the city you have neither heaven nor hell. You merely have smog overhead and pavement beneath your feet.
WILLIAM ERNEST HOCKING

You know, the more they knock New York, the bigger it gets.
WILL ROGERS

Noise is manufactured in the city, just as goods are manufactured. The city is the place where noise is kept in stock, completely detached from the object from which it came.
MAX PICARD

When it's three o'clock in New York, it's still 1938 in London.
BETTE MIDLER

The coldest winter I ever spent was a summer in San Francisco.
MARK TWAIN

New York is not Mecca, it just smells like it.
NEIL SIMON

No city should be too large for a man to walk out of in a morning.
CYRIL CONNOLLY

The lusts of the flesh can be gratified anywhere; it is not this sort of license that distinguishes New York. It is, rather, a lust of the total ego for recognition, even for eminence. More than elsewhere, everybody here wants to be Somebody.
SYDNEY J. HARRIS

New York has a trip-hammer vitality which drives you insane with restlessness if you have no inner stabilizer.
HENRY MILLER

Cities give us collision. London and New York take the nonsense out of man.
RALPH WALDO EMERSON

I have found by experience that they who have spent all their lives in cities, improve their talents but impair their virtues, and strengthen their minds but weaken their morals. CHARLES CALEB COLTON

Pigeons, those dull, unmysterious city unemployables, dressed in their grey, secondhand suits. ANTHONY CARSON

New York is the only real city-city. TRUMAN CAPOTE

The axis of the earth sticks out visibly through the centre of each and every town or city. OLIVER WENDELL HOLMES

The typical American city is in fragments—a variety of worlds wholly out of touch with each other. JOHN W. GARDNER

There is no solitude in the world like that of the big city. KATHLEEN NORRIS

To say the least, a town life makes one more tolerant and liberal in one's judgement of others. HENRY WADSWORTH LONGFELLOW

A large city cannot be experientially known; its life is too manifold for any individual to be able to participate in it. ALDOUS HUXLEY

I'd rather wake up in the middle of nowhere than in any city on earth. STEVE McQUEEN

'Tis the men, not the houses, that make the city. THOMAS FULLER

There's no more crime in New York—there's nothing left to steal. HENNY YOUNGMAN

We will neglect our cities to our peril, for in neglecting them we neglect the nation. JOHN F. KENNEDY

This is New York, a combat zone, and everyone has to have an angle or they're not allowed over the bridges or through the tunnels. Let them have their angles, it's what they live for. You've got better things to worry about, like making sure the people that actually matter don't try any funny stuff. CYNTHIA HEIMEL

Inflation

Inflation will peg
And soon will succeed
To turn your nest egg
Back to chicken feed.

Invest in inflation. It's the only thing going up. WILL ROGERS

Profits make income. Inflation makes wealth. ANON

Inflation is the one form of taxation that can be imposed without legislation. MILTON FRIEDMAN

During inflation, luxuries and necessities sell at the same price. ANON

Inflation is caused by people who believe in the romantic theory that some day wages will catch up with prices. PAUL SWEENEY

I wouldn't mind that spiral inflationary
If only my income were't so stationary. W. J. CRONCH BERGER

The good thing about inflation is that the money you haven't got isn't worth as much as it used to be. ANON

Inflation is like sin; every government denounces it and every government practices it. SIR FREDERICK LEITH-ROSS

Inflation is a fate worse than debt. JACOB M. BRAUDE

When a government spends more than it gets and when labor gets more than it gives. ROGER M. BLOUGH

Inflation: When prices that once seemed appalling now seem appealing. RAY FINE

Inflation is when you never had it so good or parted with it so fast. MAX HESS

Inflation means that last week's prices are this week's sales. ANON

Prices are going up by the elevator and wages are going up by the stairs.
ROBERT A. BEER

Deflation to cure inflation is like running over a man with a car and then, to apologize, backing up and running over him again.
SYLVIA PORTER

During inflation, talk changes from what's going on to what's going up.
ANON

Inflation? I don't know what it's all about. I don't know any more about this than an economist does, and God knows, he don't know anything.
WILL ROGERS

Inflation is like toothpaste. Once it is out, it's hard to get back in again.
ANON

If inflation continues to soar, you're going to have to work like a dog just to live like one
GEORGE GOBEL

Remember when people worried about how much it took to buy something, instead of how long?
EARL WILSON

Inflation comes from the government spending more money than it takes in. It will go away when the government stops doing that.
RONALD REAGAN

Inflation is defined as the quality that makes balloons larger and candy bars smaller.
GENERAL FEATURES CORPORATION

Inflation: When nobody has enough money because everybody has too much.
HAROLD COFFIN

During inflation your money goes half as far and gets there twice as fast.
ANON

There is just one thing I can promise you about the outer-space program. Your tax dollar will go farther.
WERNHER von BRAUN

What seems to be an eternal process in which wages chase prices, prices chase wages and both chase their past history.
CLYDE H. FARNSWORTH

Inflation is the world's most successful thief. CARL E. PERSON

The trouble with inflation is that it takes twice as much money as it used to, to live beyond our means. ANON

Inflation is paying more than the products are worth.
LEE A. DUBRIDGE

Inflation might be called prosperity with high blood pressure.
ARNOLD H. GLASGOW

It is all very well to blame inflation on the government, but isn't it caused fundamentally by our selfishness and self-indulgence?
BERNARD M. BARUCH

A dollar saved today is 75 cents earned tomorrow. JAMES RESTON

There's nothing heroic or dramatic in trying to squeeze inflation from an economy. You're trying to treat the hangover, and the fun is in the night before. DANIEL BRILL

One good thing about inflation is that the fellow who forgets his change nowadays doesn't lose half as much as he used to do. KEN HUBBARD

Inflation cannot be vanquished without effort and sacrifice. . . . There are no simple solutions, no magic wands to wave inflation away.
JIMMY CARTER

A little inflation is like a little pregnancy: it keeps growing.
LEON HENDERSON

To the office, and heard a vast amount of discussion about the inflation of currency, and for all of me they may inflate it till it bursts, or deflate it to flatness. For I have found that no matter what happens to the national currency, there is only one thing that happens to mine: it vanishes.
FRANKLIN P. ADAMS

The first panacea for a mismanaged nation is inflation of the currency: the second is war. Both bring a temporary prosperity; both bring a permanent ruin. ERNEST HEMINGWAY

Having a little inflation is like being a little pregnant. Inflation feeds on itself and quickly passes the "little" mark. DIAN COHEN

No civilized country in the world has ever voluntarily adopted the extreme philosophies of either fascism or communism, unless the middle class was first liquidated by inflation. H. W. PRENTIS

As the worth of money crumbles so does the worthiness of men. Inflation undoubtedly corrupts. GEORGE GALE

Inflation is repudiation. CALVIN COOLIDGE

Inflation is the most important fact of our time—the single greatest peril to our economic health. BERNARD M. BARUCH

Recession

And one can live cheaper than two.

The church is the only business that picks up during bad times. REVEREND CHARLES ANGEL

A recession is like an unfortunate love affair. It's a lot easier to talk your way in than it is to talk your way out. BILL VAUGHAN

In times like these it helps to recall that there have always been times like these. PAUL HARVEY

It isn't so much that hard times are coming; the change observed is mostly soft times going. GROUCHO MARX

The cost of living has gone up another dollar a quart. W. C. FIELDS

A recession is when your credit starts looking for help. ANON

It's a recession when your neighbour loses his job; it's a depression when you lose your own. HARRY S. TRUMAN

A recession is when the other guy loses his job. A depression is when you lose your job. And a panic, that's when your wife loses her job. ANON

No one has not yet found a sure way of bringing about just a little depression. ALLAN SPROUL

Slump, and the world slumps with you. Push and you push alone. ANON

A depression is a period when people do without things their parents never had. ANON

This crash is not going to have much effect on business. ARTHUR REYNOLDS

A recession is a depression that got bogged down in properity. WALT STREIGHTIFF

Everybody has a better understanding of money during a recession. ANON

If the price of duck feathers is raised, it means that down is up. JACOB M. BRAUDE

Can anybody remember when the times were not hard and money not scarce? RALPH WALDO EMERSON

Business is so quiet that you can hear the overhead pile up. ANON

There's a lot of nostalgia for the Depression, though obviously by people who didn't live through it. HILTON KRAMER

A Recession is a period in which you tighten your belt.
A Depression is a period in which you have no belt to tighten.
ANON

Checks are bouncing higher than ever. RAYMOND SCHUESSLER

My message to you is: Be courageous. I have seen many depressions in business. Always America has emerged from these stronger and more prosperous. Be brave as your fathers were before you. Have faith! Go forward! THOMAS ALVA EDISON

During a recession you discover how much money you were wasting on nonessentials. ANON

I don't know anything about any depression. J. P. MORGAN

There's nothing like a business recession to make your old clothes look like new. ANON

This would never have happened if Ronald Reagan were still President.
ANON PUNDIT on THE WALL STREET CRASH

VI METHOD

Method

In Maine or Montana
It's the same old banana;
If you do it today,
As you did yesterday,
Better watch out manana!

All I know about method is that when I am not working I sometimes think I know something, but when I am working, it is quite clear I know nothing.
JOHN CAGE

The shortest way to do many things is to do only one thing at a time.
RICHARD CECIL

The whole history of civilization is strewn with creeds and institutions which were invaluable at first, and deadly afterwards.
WALTER BAGEHOT

There is no useful rule without an exception. THOMAS FULLER

It is common sense to take a method and try it. If it fails, admit it frankly and try another. But above all, try something.
FRANKLIN D. ROOSEVELT

Systems die; instincts remain. OLIVER WENDELL HOLMES

If you think of "standardization" as the best that you know today, but which is to be improved tomorrow—you get somewhere.
HENRY FORD

A formula is something that worked once, and keeps trying to do it again.
HENRY S. HASKINS

Little by little does the trick.
AESOP

It has, I believe, been often remarked, that a hen is only an egg's way of making another egg.
SAMUEL BUTLER

The idea that to make a man work you've got to hold gold in front of his eyes is a growth, not an axiom. We've done that for so long that we've forgotten there's any other way.
F. SCOTT FITZGERALD

Many Hans make Volkswagens.
K. G. HULL

We must overcome the notion that we must be regular. . . . It robs you of the chance to be extraordinary and leads you to the mediocre.
UTA HAGEN

Any new system is worth trying when your luck is bad.
HEYWOOD BROUN

Every time you have a task before you, examine it carefully, take exact measure of what is expected of you. Then make your plan and, in order to execute it properly, create for yourself a method; never improvise.
MARSHAL FERDINAND FOCH

Fear of methodological blundering is not half so strong as fear of the consequences of doing the wrong thing.
HARRY A. BULLIS

There is time enough for everything in the course of the day if you do but one thing at once; but there is not time enough in the year if you will do two things at a time.
LORD CHESTERFIELD

We often get in quicker by the back door than by the front.
NAPOLEON BONAPARTE

A system will not die unless it is pushed aside by something else.
PIERO BASSETTI

I distrust all systematizers, and avoid them. The will to a system shows a lack of honesty. FRIEDRICH WILHELM NIETZSCHE

Method is like packing things in a box, a good packer will get in half as much again as a bad one. CECIL RICHARD

Be methodical if you would succeed in business or in anything. . . . Whatever your calling, master all its bearings and detail, its principles, instruments, and applications. Method is essential if you would get through your work easily and with economy of time.
WILLIAM MATTHEWS

A system-grinder hates the truth. RALPH WALDO EMERSON

Labels are devices for saving talkative persons the trouble of thinking.
JOHN MORLEY

No rule is so general, which admits not some exception.
ROBERT BURTON

Let every man divide his money into three parts, and invest a third in land, a third in business, and a third let him keep by him in reserve.
HEBREW PROVERB

He was gifted with the sly, sharp instinct for self-preservation that passes for wisdom among the rich. EVELYN WAUGH

Look for a tough wedge for a tough log. PUBLILIUS SYRUS

A commercial society whose members are essentially ascetic and indifferent in social ritual has to be provided with blue-prints and specifications for evoking the right tone for every occasion.
MARSHALL McLUHAN

Method will teach you to win time.
JOHANN WOLFGANG von GOETHE

To suppose that people can be saved by studying and giving assent to formulae is like supposing that one can get to Timbuctoo by poring over a map of Africa. ALDOUS LEONARD HUXLEY

There is always a best way of doing everything, if it be to boil an egg.
RALPH WALDO EMERSON

Unhappy the general who comes on the field of battle with a system.
NAPOLEON BONAPARTE

Almost all our faults are more pardonable than the methods we think up to hide them.
ANON

Dispatch is the soul of business, and nothing contributes more to Dispatch than method.
LORD CHESTERFIELD

To do two things at once is to do neither.
PUBLILIUS SYRUS

Be methodical if you would succeed in business, or in anything. Have a work for every moment, and mind the moment's work. Whatever your calling, master all its bearings and details, its principles, instruments, and applications. Method is essential if you would get through your work easily and with economy of time.
WILLIAM MATHEWS

Method is the very hinge of business; and there is no method without punctuality.
RICHARD CECIL

Our systems, perhaps, are nothing more than an unconscious apology for our faults—a gigantic scaffolding whose object is to hide from us our favorite sin.
HENRI FREDERIC AMIEL

There nearly always is method in madness. It's what drives men mad, being methodical.
GILBERT KEITH CHESTERTON

What sets us against one another is not our aims—they all come to the same thing—but our methods, which are the fruit of our varied reasoning.
ANTOINE de SAINT-EXUPERY

One arrow does not bring down two birds.
TURKISH PROVERB

Attempt easy tasks as if they were difficult, and difficult as if they were easy; in the one case that confidence may not fall asleep, in the other that it may not be dismayed.
BALTASAR GRACIAN

It is best to do things systematically, since we are only human, and disorder is our worst enemy.
HESIOD

Method goes far to prevent trouble in business; for it makes the task easy, hinders confusion, saves abundance of time, and instructs those who have business depending, what to do and what to hope.
WILLIAM PENN

Better one safe way than a hundred on which you cannot reckon.
AESOP

Method facilitates every kind of business, and by making it easy makes it agreeable, and also successful. CHARLES SIMMONS

To touch a man's heart, sympathize with him;
To touch a man's wallet, flatter him. ANON

Judgment

Good judgement comes
From experience;
Experience comes
From poor judgement.

Timing is the chief ingredient in judgment. WILLIAM FEATHER

The man who called it "near beer" was a bad judge of distance.
PHILANDER JOHNSON

Snap judgment has a way of becoming unfastened. ANON

A declaration that "science has discovered" has been for Americans a final judgment to which there is no court of appeal. DAVID F. MUSTO

The need to dominate can affect one's judgement. ANON

Gone With the Wind is going to be the biggest flop in Hollywood history.
GARY COOPER

Statistics are no substitute for judgment. EDMUND FULLER

Don't judge everything by appearances, the early bird may simply have been up all night. ANON

A man cannot administer great corporations which employ armies of men and serve large communities if his judgment is diluted and distracted by huge speculative transactions. A man cannot be a good doctor and keep telephoning to his broker between visits to his patients, nor a good lawyer with one eye on the ticker. WALTER LIPPMAN

Of what possible commercial importance can Alaska be to us?
ORANGE FERRIS

The best investments are often those that looked dead wrong when they were made. ANON

Most people suspend their judgment till somebody else has expressed his own and then they repeat it. ERNEST DIMNET

Precipitate judgment brings swift regret. LATIN PROVERB

We don't think the Beatles will do anything in this market.
PRESIDENT OF CAPITOL RECORDS

In judging others, folks will work overtime with no pay.
CHARLES EDWIN CARRUTHERS

The reason why many persons don't see things in the right perspective is that they are always looking for an angle. ANON

Every man prefers belief to the exercise of judgment.
LUCIUS SENECA

I mistrust the judgment of every man in a case in which his own wishes are concerned. DUKE of WELLINGTON

Good and bad luck is but a synonym, in the great majority of instances, for good and bad judgment. ANON

It is with our judgments as with our watches; no two go just alike, yet each believes his own. ALEXANDER POPE

The cobbler should not judge beyond his last.
CAIUS P. SECUNDUS PLINY

Judge not the play before the play be done. SIR JOHN DAVIES

Choice has always been a privilege of those who could afford to pay for it. ELLEN FRANKFORT

We easily enough confess in others an advantage of courage, strength, experience, activity, and beauty: but an advantage in judgment we yield to none. MICHEL de MONTAIGNE

A mistake in judgment isn't fatal, but too much anxiety about judgment is. PAULINE KAEL

Where two Jews, three opinions. ANON

A racing tipster who only reached Hitler's level of accuracy would not do well for his clients. ALAN JOHN PERCIVALE TAYLOR

Uncertainty kills business. SIR MICHAEL EDWARDS

Sentence first—verdict afterwards. LEWIS CARROLL

Don't hear one and judge two. GREEK PROVERB

Judge not, that ye be not judged. *Matthew*

One cool judgment is worth a thousand hasty councils. THOMAS WOODROW WILSON

People are so overwhelmed with the prestige of their instruments that they consider their personal judgment of hardly any account. WYNDHAM LEWIS

The ultimate cynicism is to suspend judgment so that you are not judged. MARYA MANNES

Planning

It's a fallacy
To plan too far
That times will be
The way they are

Life is what happens to us while we are making other plans. ALLEN SAUNDERS

The plans
Are man's;
The odds
Are God's. KUAN FEI

It's astonishing in this world how things don't turn out at all the way you expect them to! AGATHA CHRISTIE

Never make forecasts, especially about the future. SAMUEL GOLDWYN

Every man has a scheme that won't work. EDGAR WATSON HOWE

Don't ever prophesy, for if you prophesy wrong, nobody will forget it, and if you prophesy right, nobody will remember it. JOSH BILLINGS

Luck is what happens when preparation meets opportunity. ELMER G. LETERMAN

Real life seems to have no plots. IVY COMPTON-BURNETT

Before everything else, getting ready is the secret of success. HENRY FORD

We have enough people who tell it like it is—now we could use a few who tell it like it can be. ROBERT ORBEN

Who is not ready today, will not be ready tomorrow. ENGLISH PROVERB

Bite off more than you can chew,
Then chew it.
Plan more than you can do,
Then do it. ANON

The farther backward you can look, the farther forward you are likely to see. SIR WINSTON CHURCHILL

Insanity consists of building major structures upon foundations which do not exist. NORMAN MAILER

Nearly all the best things that came to me in life have been unexpected, unplanned by me CARL SANDBURG

Make no little plans Think big. CLARENCE FRANCIS

There are no small steps in great affairs. CARDINAL de RETZ

Amid a multitude of projects, no plan is devised. PUBLILIUS SYRUS

The conscientious plodder is nearly always outdistanced by the fellow who stops occasionally to analyze and plan. W. J. CAMERON

Those most dedicated to the future are not always the best prophets. ELINOR HAYS

You have to be flexible. If you have a plan and just blindly follow it, it's worse than no plan at all. L. F. McCOLLUM

In all matters one must consider the end. JEAN de la FONTAINE

Prepare for the worst and be equal to it. IAN FERGUSON

Don't be afraid to take a big step if one is indicated, you can't cross a chasm in two small jumps. DAVID LLOYD GEORGE

Do not plan for ventures before finishing what's at hand. EURIPIDES

The unexpected always happens. LAURENCE J. PETER

He who can see three days ahead will be rich for three thousand years. JAPANESE PROVERB

There is many a slip 'twixt the cup and the lip. WILLIAM HAZLITT

It doesn't matter how small you are if you have faith and a plan of action. FIDEL CASTRO

For man plans, but God arranges. THOMAS à KEMPIS

Urgent necessity prompts many to do things, at the very thoughts of which they perhaps would start at other times. MIGUEL de CERVANTES

We must not waste life in devising means. It is better to plan less and do more. WILLIAM ELLERY CHANNING

Nothing is more terrible than activity without insight. THOMAS CARLYLE

Beware of false prophets, which come to you in sheep's clothing, but inwardly they are ravening wolves. *Matthew*

It is a mistake to look too far ahead. Only one link in the chain of destiny can be handled at a time. SIR WINSTON CHURCHILL

Don't ever prophesy—unless ye know. JAMES RUSSELL LOWELL

Prepare yourself for the great world, as the athletes used to do for their exercises; oil your mind and your manners, to give them the necessary suppleness and flexibility; strength alone will not do, as young people are too apt to think. LORD CHESTERFIELD

The best laid plans o' mice an' men
Gang aft agley,
An' lea'e us nought but grief an' pain,
For promised joy! ROBERT BURNS

The strength of any plan depends on timing.
MICHEL de MONTAIGNE

Magnificently unprepared
For the long littleness of life. FRANCES CORNFORD

Enterprise

You have to enter
To win the prize.

Getting there isn't half the fun—it's all the fun. ROBERT TOWNSEND

If you do not do so yourself, someone else will.
ARTHUR B. DOUGALL

There are two ways to get to the top of an oak tree—you can climb it or you can sit on an acorn. R. FRANK BROWN

Destiny leads the willing, but drags the unwilling. THOMAS FULLER

To make dough, do. BERTRAM TROY

If the Treasury were to fill old bottles with banknotes, bury them at suitable depths in disused coalmines which are then filled up to the surface with town rubbish, and leave it to private enterprise on well-tried principles of laissez-faire to dig the notes up again—there need be no more unemployment and, with the help of the repercussions, the real income of the community would probably become a good deal larger than it actually is. J. MAYNARD KEYNES

!!! One shoe shined absolutely free !!! ANONYMOUS SIGN

I believe in getting into hot water; it keeps you clean.
GILBERT KEITH CHESTERTON

Stupid sons don't ruin a family; it is the clever ones who do.
MR. TUT-TUT

The average man is always waiting for something to happen to him instead of setting to work to make it happen. For one person who dreams of making fifty thousand pounds, a hundred people dream of being left fifty thousand pounds. ALAN ALEXANDER MILNE

Why not go out on a limb? Isn't that where the fruit is?
FRANK SCULLY

Nothing is ever accomplished by a reasonable man. FRED BUCY

We always ski on the higher slopes when we can. WILLIAM H. GASS

Be a pianist not a piano. A. R. ORAGE

Any jackass can kick down a barn, but it takes a good carpenter to build one. SAM RAYBURN

Beware of all enterprises that require new clothes.
HENRY DAVID THOREAU

Discovery consists of seeing what everybody has seen and thinking what nobody has thought. A. SZENT-GYORGYI

If you take big paces you leave big spaces. BURMESE PROVERB

It's not a question of who's going to throw the first stone; it's a question of who's going to start building with it. SLOAN WILSON

Only the game fish swims upstream. JOHN TROTWOOD MOORE

It is so tempting to try the most difficult thing possible.
JENNIE JEROME CHURCHILL

It is Enterprise which builds and improves the world's possessions. If Enterprise is afoot, wealth accumulates, whatever may be happening to Thrift; and if Enterprise is asleep, Wealth decays, whatever Thrift may be doing. JOHN MAYNARD KEYNES

The spur of the moment is the essence of adventure.
ANTHONY ARMSTRONG-JONES

All profoundly original work looks ugly at first.
CLEMENT GREENBERG

If you dip your arm into the picklepot let it be up to the elbow.
MALAY PROVERB

Remember the turtle progresses only when he sticks out his neck.
ANON

Doing just the opposite is also a form of imitation.
GEORG CHRISTOPH LICHTENBERG

On the neck of the young man sparkles no gem so gracious as enterprise.
HAFIZ

In every enterprise consider where you would come out.
PUBLILIUS SYRUS

Men are always averse to enterprises in which they foresee difficulties.
NICCOLO MACHIAVELLI

The method of the enterprising is to plan with audacity, and execute with vigor; to sketch out a map of possibilities, and then to treat them as probabilities. CHRISTIAN NESTELL BOVEE

Many great things indeed have been achieved by those who chose not to leap into the mainstream. JOAN MONDALE

In order to carry out great enterprises, one must live as if one will never have to die. MARQUIS de VAUVENARGUES

Gullibility is the key to all adventures. The greenhorn is the ultimate victor in everything; it is he that gets the most out of life.
GILBERT KEITH CHESTERTON

Every man did that which was right in his own eyes. *Judges*

Believe me, the enterprise that begins with a prayer will end with prosperity, fame and triumph. HEINRICH von KLEIST

Ideas

The very first thing to do
With an idea when you get it
Is to make quite sure that you
Don't immediately forget it.

The man with a new idea is a crank until the idea succeeds.
MARK TWAIN

It is with ideas, as with umbrellas, if left lying about they are peculiarly liable to a change of ownership. ANON

Ideas pull the trigger, but instinct loads the gun.
DONALD ROBERT PERRY MARQUIS

If you can explain it, it's not worth doing. DAVID THOMAS

It is more important that a proposition be interesting than that it be true.
ALFRED NORTH WHITEHEAD

A man must let his ideas grow, not be continually rooting them up to see how they are getting on. WILLIAM McFEE

The essence of success is that it is never necessary to think of a new idea. It is far better to wait until somebody else does it, and then to copy him in every detail except his mistakes. AUBREY MENEN

It's unpleasant to be able to turn certain ideas over in your mind that nobody suspects you of having. UGO BETTI

Every man with an idea has at least two or three followers.
BROOKS ATKINSON

Our ideas are for the most part like bad sixpences, and we spend our lives in trying to pass them on one another. SAMUEL BUTLER

Ideas buzzed like a swarm without a hive. PETER DE VRIES

What we need is hatred—from it are our ideas born. JEAN GENET

Daring ideas are like chessmen moved forward. They may be beaten but they may start a winning game. JOHANN WOLFGANG von GOETHE

When we are tired, we are attacked by ideas we conquered long ago.
FRIEDRICH WILHELM NIETZSCHE

A powerful idea communicates some of its power to the man who contradicts it. MARCEL PROUST

Crazy people with only a single idea are the men who make things move; but they are not nice to talk to. RUDYARD KIPLING

In many ways ideas are more important than people—they are much more permanent. CHARLES F. KETTERING

An idea isn't worth much until a man is found who has the energy and ability to make it work. WILLIAM FEATHER

If you have a bright idea and you do the right kind of experiment, you may get pretty decisive results pretty soon.
PROFESSOR WILLIAM B. SHOCKLEY

If we watch ourselves honestly, we shall often find that we have begun to argue against a new idea even before it has been completely stated.
ARTHUR KOESTLER

Only constant repetition will finally succeed in imprinting an idea on the memory of the crowd. ADOLF HITLER

Man's fear of ideas is probably the greatest dike holding back human knowledge and happiness. MORRIS L. ERNST

An idea is not so powerless that it cannot make itself into more than an idea. FRIEDRICH HEGEL

You can't achieve anything without getting in someone's way. You can't be detached and effective. ABBA EBAN

What matters is not the idea a man holds, but the depth at which he holds it. EZRA POUND

Every new idea has something of the pain and peril of childbirth about it. SAMUEL BUTLER

Keep a secret, it's your slave. Tell it, and it's your master. WILL HENRY

One of the greatest pains to human nature is the pain of a new idea. WALTER BAGEHOT

The wise only possess ideas; the greater part of mankind are possessed by them. SAMUEL TAYLOR COLERIDGE

All erroneous ideas would perish of their own accord if given clear expression. MARQUIS de VAUVENARGUES

A new idea is delicate. It can be killed by a sneer or a yawn; it can be stabbed to death by a quip and worried to death by a frown on the nightman's brow. CHARLES BROWER

Learn to love ideas for themselves; and do not think, the instant a truth dawns on you, of devising a scheme for reforming the world. JOHN LANCASTER SPALDING

The mark of highest originality lies in the ability to develop a familiar idea so fruitfully that it would seem no one else would ever have discovered so much to be hidden in it. JOHANN WOLFGANG von GOETHE

You must find the ideas that have some promise in them. It is not enough to just have ideas, they must be finally ideas worth having and fruitful. GEORGE E. WOODBERRY

It is desirable at times for ideas to possess a certain roughness, like drawings on heavy-grain paper. Thoughts having this quality are most likely to match the texture of actual experience. HAROLD ROSENBERG

You cannot put a rope around the neck of an idea; you cannot put an idea up against a barrack square wall and riddle it with bullets; you cannot confine it in the strongest prison cell that your slaves could ever build.
SEAN O'CASEY

Never, never rest contented with any circle of ideas, but always be certain that a wider one is still possible. RICHARD JEFFERIES

The vitality of thought is an adventure. Ideas won't keep. Something must be done about them. When the idea is new, its custodians have fervor, live for it, and if need be, die for it.
ALFRED NORTH WHITEHEAD

Ideas and opinions, like living organisms, have a normal rate of growth which cannot be either checked or forced beyond a certain point.
SAMUEL BUTLER

More than 30 patents have been issued on inventions designed to extract gold from seawater. L. M. BOYD

"Dying for an idea," again, sounds well enough, but why not let the idea die instead of you? PERCY WYNDHAM LEWIS

The insolence of authority is endeavoring to substitute money for ideas.
FRANK LLOYD WRIGHT

A fellow has come up with a sure money-maker to reach the teen-age market—he wants to put jukeboxes in phone booths. EARL WILSON

It is easy to overlook the absence of appreciable advance in an industry. Inventions that are not made, like babies that are not born, are rarely missed. JOHN KENNETH GALBRAITH

One should operate by dissociation, and not by association, of ideas. An association is almost always commonplace. Dissociation decomposes, and uncovers latent affinities. JULES RENARD

It is the nature of an hypothesis, when once a man has conceived it, that it assimilates every thing to itself as proper nourishment, and from the first moment of your begetting it, it generally grows the stronger by every thing you see, hear, read, or understand. LAURENCE STERNE

Defeat is a fact and victory can be a fact. If the idea is good, it will survive defeat, it may even survive the victory.
STEPHEN VINCENT BENET

Those ideas which are least our own, are the ones most easily expressed in language.
HENRI BERGSON

Every great idea exerts, on first appearing, a tyrannical influence: hence the advantages it brings are turned all too soon into disadvantages.
JOHANN WOLFGANG von GOETHE

Opportunity

Weak men wait for them;
Strong men take them;
The best men make them.

Opportunity: A favorable occasion for grasping a disappointment.
AMBROSE BIERCE

The fact is, nothing comes; at least, nothing good. All has to be fetched.
CHARLES BUXTON

I had a terrible thing happen to me yesterday. Opportunity knocked on my door and by the time I unhooked the chain, pushed back the bolt, turned the two locks, and shut off the burglar alarm—it was gone!
ROBERT ORBEN

An opportunist is any man who goes ahead and does what you always intended to do.
KENNETH L. KRICHBAUM

Every French soldier carries in his cartridge-pouch the baton of a marshal of France.
NAPOLEON BONAPARTE

There are really only three types of people: those who make things happen, those who watch things happen, and those who say, "What happened?"
ANN LANDERS

I'm not the kind of a guy to knock at a door and then when the door is opened not go in. WILLIAM SAROYAN

It is a good idea to take things as they come—if you can handle them that fast. SIG ARNO

Things don't turn up in this world until somebody turns them up. JAMES A. GARFIELD

As many as 100 pearls have been found in a single oyster. L. M. BOYD

You say, "Here is the opportunity," and the youth of America says, "How much are you going to pay me?" CASEY STENGEL

When you are genuinely interested in one thing it will always lead to something else. ELEANOR ROOSEVELT

The Gods cannot help those who do not seize opportunities. CONFUCIUS

The best you get is an even break. ANON

A pessimist is one who makes difficulties of his opportunities; an optimist is one who makes opportunities of his difficulties. VICE-ADMIRAL MANSELL

Half the pleasure of life consists of the opportunities one has neglected. OLIVER WENDELL HOLMES

Next to knowing when to seize an opportunity, the most important thing in life is to know when to forgo an advantage. BENJAMIN DISRAELI

A great many men—some comparatively small men now—if put in the right position, would be Luthers and Columbuses. EDWIN HUBBELL CHAPIN

When one door closes, another opens, but we often look so long and so regretfully upon the closed door that we do not see the one which has opened for us. ALEXANDER GRAHAM BELL

Everyone must row with the oars he has. ENGLISH PROVERB

Poor people are not poor because they're dumb or because they're lazy but because society has not provided opportunity. ANDREW YOUNG

Seize opportunity by the beard, for it is bald behind.
BULGARIAN PROVERB

When a resolute young fellow steps up to the great bully, the world, and takes him boldly by the beard, he is often surprised to find that the beard comes off in his hand, that it was only tied on to scare away timid adventurers. OLIVER WENDELL HOLMES

God gives every bird its food, but he does not throw it into the nest.
J. G. HOLLAND

An optimist sees an opportunity in every calamity; a pessimist sees a calamity in every opportunity. SIR WINSTON CHURCHILL

Roasted pigeons will not fly into one's mouth.
PENNSYLVANIA DUTCH PROVERB

Democracy is like a hobby horse; it will carry you nowhere unless you use your own legs. LORD SAMUEL

Take what you want, said God; take it and pay for it.
OLD SPANISH PROVERB

The opportunities of man are limited only by his imagination. But so few have imagination that there are ten thousand fiddlers to one composer.
CHARLES F. KETTERING

It is better to have a hen today than an egg tomorrow.
THOMAS FULLER

God gives no linen, but flax to spin. GERMAN PROVERB

The bell never rings of itself; unless someone handles or moves it, it is dumb. PLAUTUS

There is a tide in the affairs of men,
Which, taken at the flood, leads on to fortune,
Omitted, all the voyage of their life
Is bound in shallows and in miseries,
On such a full sea are we now afloat;
And we must take the current when it serves,
Or lose our ventures. WILLIAM SHAKESPEARE

Contracts

Read every contract clause right through,
You'll regret it if you don't;
You will gain knowledge when you do
And experience when you won't.

In every contract the big print giveth and the small print taketh away.
ANON

A Gentleman's Agreement is an arrangement which is not an agreement between two persons, neither of whom are gentlemen, with each expecting the other to be strictly bound while he himself has no intention of being bound at all.
MR. JUSTICE VALSEY

Now as through this world I ramble,
I see lots of funny men,
Some rob you with a six gun,
Some with a fountain pen.
WOODY GUTHRIE

In a fifty-fifty deal, some negotiators insist on the hyphen as well.
ANON

The hand that gives is above the hand that takes.
TURKISH PROVERB

I just bought a new life insurance policy but the small print is hard to understand. All I'm sure of is that after I die I can stop paying.
LEOPOLD FECHTNER

The older you are the more slowly you read a contract.
ANON

Treaties are like roses and young girls. They last while they last.
CHARLES de GAULLE

Contract: an agreement that is binding only on the weaker party.
FREDERICK SAWYER

Why is it that goods sent by ship are called a cargo, when goods sent by road are called a shipment?
ANON

Never co-sign.
AL McGUIRE

A verbal contract isn't worth the paper it's written on.
SAMUEL GOLDWYN

Any time a man can't come and settle with you without bringing his lawyer—look out for him. WILL ROGERS

There's no hiding place in better use than small print. ANON

One of the mysteries of human conduct is why adult men and women are ready to sign documents which they do not read, at the behest of canvassers whom they do not know, binding them to pay for articles which they do not want, with money which they have not got.
SIR GERALD HURST

Drink nothing without seeing it, sign nothing without reading it.
SPANISH PROVERB

I start worrying about losing an account the minute I get it. The minute I sign the contract, I'm one step closer to losing it.
JERRY DELLA FEMINA

A bad agreement is better than a good lawsuit. ITALIAN PROVERB

Joint undertakings stand a better chance
When they benefit both sides EURIPIDES

Treaties are like piecrust. They are made to be broken.
NIKOLAI LENIN

Nothing was ever promised you. You signed no contract.
CHARLES BUKOWSKI

Not every bargain clear and plain
That none may afterwards complain. EDMUND FULLER

Treaties are observed as long as they are in harmony.
NAPOLEON BONAPARTE

The plainest print cannot be read through a gold eagle.
ABRAHAM LINCOLN

The first principle of a civilized state is that the power is legitimate only when it is under contract. WALTER LIPPMAN

Who ties well, unties well. SPANISH PROVERB

Bargaining

A bargain is never ideal
And the loser is he who forgets it;
It may take only two to deal
But it's usually one that gets it.

A bargain is something you buy today at yesterday's prices. ANON

There are very honest people who do not think that they have had a bargain unless they have cheated a merchant. ANATOLE FRANCE

Be bold when you've got a hot hand. CHARLES H. KIRBO

Never give a sucker an Even Break. W. C. FIELDS

Man is the animal that bargains; no dogs exchange bones.
ADAM SMITH

A bargain is something you have to find a use for once you have bought it. BENJAMIN FRANKLIN

The owner of a second-hand car knows how hard it is to drive a bargain.
Banking

If Max Beaverbrook gets to Heaven he won't last long. He will be chucked out for trying to pull off a merger between Heaven and Hell, after having secured a controlling interest in key subsidiary companies in both places, of course. HERBERT GEORGE WELLS

Never tell them what you wouldn't do. ADAM CLAYTON POWELL

Bargains made in speed are commonly repented at leisure.
GEORGE PETTIE

A bargain is a disease caught in the Sunday papers and developed in department stores on Mondays. ANON

Once you pledge, don't hedge. NIKITA KHRUSHCHEV

It is impossible to persuade a man who does not disagree, but smiles.
MURIEL SPARK

The chances are about ten to one that the person who slaps you on the back is trying to make you cough up something. OLIN MILLER

A bargain sale is when a woman ruins one dress while buying another. ANON

A little sincerity is a dangerous thing, and a great deal of it is absolutely fatal. OSCAR WILDE

It is a bad bargain when both are losers. EDMUND FULLER

Magnificent promises are always to be suspected. THEODORE PARKER

A stone thrown at the right time is better than gold given at the wrong time. PERSIAN PROVERB

With a gentleman I am always a gentleman and a half, and with a fraud I try to be a fraud and a half. OTTO EDUARD LEOPOLD von BISMARCK

Do not assume that the other fellow has intelligence to match yours. He may have more. TERRY THOMAS

Look out for the fellow who lets you do all the talking. FRANK McKINNEY HUBBARD

Whenever you buy or sell let or hire, make a definite bargain, and never trust to the flattering lie, "We shan't disagree about trifles." ANON

Be a hypocrite if you like, but don't talk like one! DENIS DIDEROT

It's going to be a tough decision when the purchasing agent starts negotiating to buy the machine that's to replace him. DAVE MURRAY

We all like a man who comes right out and says what he thinks—when he agrees with us. ANON

Moderation is commonly firm, and firmness is commonly successful. SAMUEL JOHNSON

Looking at bargains from a purely commercial point of view, someone is always cheated, but looked at with the simple eye both seller and buyer always win. DAVID GRAYSON

Don't take action because of a name. A name is an uncertain thing. You can't count on it. BERTOLT BRECHT

You must lose a fly to catch a trout. GEORGE HERBERT

Here's the rule for bargains: "Do other men, for they would do you." That's the true business concept. CHARLES DICKENS

If your opponent proposes an alteration, you can call it an innovation. If you are making the proposal, it will be the other way round. ARTHUR SCHOPENHAUER

Overcome shyness, and help yourself make it in your world! Ask the dealer, "How much is your realistic bottom price?" After you hear it, you already have saved a good bit in case you buy. ROY M. COHN

A disagreement may be the shortest cut between two minds. KAHLIL GIBRAN

He that promises too much means nothing. THOMAS FULLER

When you have given nothing, ask for nothing. ALBANIAN PROVERB

Civility is not a sign of weakness, and sincerity is always subject to proof. JOHN F. KENNEDY

Sometimes it's necessary to go a long distance out of the way in order to come back a short distance correctly. EDWARD ALBEE

No man is good for anything who has not some particle of obstinacy to use upon occasion. HENRY WARD BEECHER

Bargain like a gypsy, but pay like a gentleman. PROVERB

Malice is like a game of poker or tennis; you don't play it with someone who is manifestly inferior to you. HILDE SPIEL

The body pays for a slip of the foot, and gold pays for a slip of the tongue. MALAY PROVERB

One man's cliché can be another man's conviction. ADLAI STEVENSON

Suit your manner to the man. PUBLIUS TERENTIUS TERENCE

We must not promise what we ought not, lest we be called upon to perform what we cannot. ABRAHAM LINCOLN

Better deny at once than promise long. DANISH PROVERB

When firmness is sufficient, rashness is unnecessary.
NAPOLEON BONAPARTE

Delay is a great procuress. OVID

You never know what is enough unless you know what is more than enough. WILLIAM BLAKE

A man surprised is half beaten. THOMAS FULLER

The ability to get to the verge without getting into the war is the necessary art. JOHN FOSTER DULLES

Men are all alike in their promises. It is only in their deeds they differ.
JEAN BAPTISTE MOLIÈRE

A miser and a liar bargain quickly. GREEK PROVERB

Be slow of tongue and quick of eye. MIGUEL de CERVANTES

Much truth is spoken, that more may be concealed.
MR. JUSTICE DARLING

Luck

We talk about the good luck
Of that famous early bird
But never of the bad luck
Of the poor old early worm.

Good luck beats early rising. IRISH PROVERB

Some folk want their luck buttered. THOMAS HARDY

I am a great believer in luck, and I find the harder I work the more I have it. STEPHEN LEACOCK

A guy once stooped to pick up a horseshoe and a car hit him into a field of four-leafed clover. ANON

Some people are so fond of ill-luck that they run half-way to meet it. DOUGLAS JERROLD

Depend on the rabbit's foot if you will, but remember it didn't work for the rabbit! R. E. SHAY

If it weren't for bad luck, I wouldn't have had no luck at all! DICK GREGORY

The only good luck many great men ever had was being born with the ability and determination to overcome bad luck. CHANNING POLLOCK

Good luck is a lazy man's estimate of a worker's success. ANON

Luck is loaned, not owned. YIDDISH PROVERB

Fortune is always on the side of the largest battalions. MARIE de RABUTIN-CHANTAL

A man does not seek his luck, luck seeks its man. TURKISH PROVERB

If it rained soup, he'd have a fork. ANON

The cult of heroes is the cult of luck. LOUIS-FERDINAND CELINE

Do not be born good or handsome, but be born lucky. RUSSIAN PROVERB

Just say that I was shot in the ass with luck. DONALD OGDEN STEWART

It is a very bad thing to become accustomed to good luck. PUBLILIUS SYRUS

Watch out w'en you er gittin' all you want. Fattening hogs ain't in luck. JOEL CHANDLER HARRIS

Good luck only happens to people who do things, not to those who sit around and hope. ANON

As for what you're calling hard luck—well, we made New England out of it, that and codfish. STEPHEN VINCENT BENET

Those who mistake their good luck for their merit are inevitably bound for disaster. J. CHRISTOPHER HEROLD

A great man's greatest good luck is to die at the right time. ERIC HOFFER

It would seem that you don't be having any good luck until you believe there is no such thing as luck in it at all. IRISH PROVERB

Who has good luck is good
Who has bad luck is bad. BERTOLT BRECHT

The only sure thing about luck is that it will change. BRET HARTE

Whenever you can, hang around the lucky. JEWISH PROVERB

Throw a lucky man into the sea, and he will come up with a fish in his mouth. ARABIC PROVERB

You can't hope to be lucky. You have to prepare to be lucky. TIMOTHY DOWD

If you were born lucky, even your rooster will lay eggs. RUSSIAN PROVERB

Luck sometimes visits a fool, but never sits down with him. GERMAN PROVERB

Some men never find prosperity, for all their voyaging, while others find it with no voyaging. EURIPIDES

Good luck beats early rising. IRISH PROVERB

Luck and strength go together When you get lucky you have to have the strength to follow through. You also have to have the strength to wait for the luck. MARIO PUZO

There is no such thing as luck. It's a fancy name for being always at our duty, and so sure to be ready when the good time comes.

CHANNING POLLOCK

Bad luck is fertile.

RUSSIAN PROVERB

If fortune smiles, who doesn't? If fortune doesn't, who does?

CHINESE PROVERB

A clever man can turn bad luck to his advantage but a fool can turn even good luck to his disadvantage.

FRANCOIS DUC de la ROCHEFOUCAULD

Never have anything to do with an unlucky place, or an unlucky man. I have seen many clever men, very clever men, who had not shoes to their feet. I never act with them. Their advice sounds very well, but they cannot get on themselves; and if they cannot do good to themselves, how can they do good to me?

MAYER A. ROTHSCHILD

Fortune brings in some boats that are not steered.

WILLIAM SHAKESPEARE

Luck is the residue of design.

BRANCH RICKEY

Be grateful for luck, but don't depend on it.

WILLIAM FEATHER

It is a great piece of skill to know how to guide your luck even while waiting for it.

BALTASAR GRACIAN

Luck, bad if not good, will always be with us. But it has a way of favoring the intelligent and showing its back to the stupid.

JOHN DEWEY

The lucky man's enemy dies, and the unlucky man's friend.

RUSSIAN PROVERB

Fate is not an eagle, it creeps like a rat.

ELIZABETH BOWEN

Fortune's expensive smile is earned.

IRISH PROVERB

Fortune is a woman; if you neglect her today do not expect to regain her tomorrow.

FRENCH PROVERB

Shallow men believe in luck, wise and strong men in cause and effect.

RALPH WALDO EMERSON

We should manage our fortunes as we do our health—enjoy it when good, be patient when it is bad, and never apply violent remedies except in an extreme necessity. FRANCOIS DUC de la ROCHEFOUCAULD

People who believe they're going to have good luck and find the answer usually do find it because they've put the idea of their success into their subconscious. BILL LEAR

Behind bad luck comes good luck. GYPSY PROVERB

Little is the luck I've had,
And oh, 'tis comfort small
To think that many another lad
Has had no luck at all. ALFRED EDWARD HOUSMAN

Henceforth I ask not good fortune, I myself am good fortune.
WALT WHITMAN

Go and wake up your luck. PERSIAN PROVERB

Have but luck, and you will have the rest; be fortunate and you will be thought great. VICTOR HUGO

VII RISK

Risk

When you insure
All you are getting
Is a mature
Method of betting.

There's no such thing as "zero risk." WILLIAM DRIVER

Whatever you have, you must either use or lose. HENRY FORD

In the bad old days . . . there were three easy ways of losing money, racing being the quickest, women the pleasantest and farming the most certain. LORD AMHURST of HACKNEY

During the first period of a man's life the greatest danger is: not to take the risk. SOREN KIERKEGAARD

The worst financial risks are those that think the world owes them a living. ANON

Take calculated risks. That is quite different from being rash. GEN. GEORGE SMITH PATTON

A pinch of probability is worth a pound of perhaps. JAMES THURBER

Insurance is death on the installment plan. PHILIP SLATER

To win you have to risk loss. JEAN-CLAUDE KILLY

A man sits as many risks as he runs. HENRY DAVID THOREAU

The oil business, you know, is liable to sudden and violent fluctuations.
JOHN D. ROCKEFELLER

Be wary of the man who urges an action in which he himself incurs no risk. JOAQUIN SETANTI

Whoever plays deep must necessarily lose his money or his character.
EARL OF CHESTERFIELD

He who does not open his eyes must open his purse.
GERMAN PROVERB

Insurance is a guarantee that, no matter how many necessities a person has to forgo all through life, death was something to which he could look forward. FRED ALLEN

Progress means taking risks, for you can't steal home and keep your foot on third base. HERBERT V. PROCHNOW

Being grown up means we can have our own way—at our expense.
HAL ROGERS

There is only one thing about which I am certain, and that is that there is very little about which one can be certain.
WILLIAM SOMERSET MAUGHAM

To be alive at all involves some risk. HAROLD MACMILLAN

If at first you do succeed, don't take any more chances.
FRANK McKINNEY HUBBARD

In putting off what one has to do, one runs the risk of never being able to do it. CHARLES BEAUDELAIRE

Not every bullet kills. ALPHONSE DAUDET

There are risks and costs to a program of action. But they are far less than the long-range risks and costs of comfortable inaction.
JOHN F. KENNEDY

Risk is essential. There is no growth or inspiration in staying within what is safe and comfortable. Once you find out what you do best, why not try something else? ALEX NOBLE

Hope is a risk that must be run. GEORGE BERNARD SHAW

Danger can never be overcome without taking risks. LATIN PROVERB

We can be absolutely certain only about things we do not understand.
ERIC HOFFER

Rashness succeeds often, still more often fails.
NAPOLEON BONAPARTE

First weigh the considerations, then take the risks.
HELMUTH von MOLTKE

The profits of good luck are perishable; if you build on fortune, you build on sand; the more advancement you achieve, the more dangers you run.
MARQUIS de RACAN

Every man has the right to risk his own life in order to save it.
JEAN-JACQUES ROUSSEAU

If you dip your arm into the pickle pot, let it be up to the elbow.
MALAY PROVERB

If you leap into a well, providence is not bound to fetch you out.
THOMAS FULLER

To win without risk is to triumph without glory. PIERRE CORNEILLE

Risk! Risk anything! Care no more for the opinions of others, for those voices. Do the hardest thing on earth for you. Act for yourself.
KATHERINE MANSFIELD

To get profit without risk, experience without danger, and reward without work, is as impossible as it is to live without being born.
A. P. GOUTHEY

Chance

There's a little bit of chance
In every circumstance;
There are football fumbles,
The way the cookie crumbles,
There's either and or,
The luck of the draw,
There are accidents,
And coincidence.
But it's one of God's laws
That nothing is without cause.

Luck is being ready for the chance. J. FRANK DOBIE

The man who leaves nothing to chance will do few things badly, but he will do very few things. GEORGE SAVILE HALIFAX

No one ever stumbled on something sitting down. ANON

Chance is perhaps the pseudonym of God when He did not want to sign. ANATOLE FRANCE

Fortune rarely accompanies anyone to the door. BALTASAR GRACIAN

Chance does nothing that has not been prepared beforehand. ALEXIS de TOCQUEVILLE

We make our fortunes, and we call them fate. DAVID ALROY

I have always believed that all things depended upon Fortune and nothing upon ourselves. LORD GEORGE GORDON NOEL BYRON

No victor believes in chance. FRIEDRICH WILHELM NIETZSCHE

Chance makes a football of a man's life. LUCIUS ANNAEUS SENECA

As much chance as a one-armed blind man in a dark room trying to shove a pound of melted butter into a wildcat's left ear with a red hot needle. PELHAM GRENVILLE WODEHOUSE

If there is anything that a man can do and do well, I say let him do it. Give him a chance. ABRAHAM LINCOLN

Take a chance! All life is a chance. The man who goes furthest is generally the one who is willing to do and dare. The "sure thing" boat never gets far from shore. DALE CARNEGIE

Good or bad fortune usually comes to those who have more of the one than the other. FRANCOIS DUC de la ROCHEFOUCAULD

To put one's trust in God is only a longer way of saying that one will chance it. SAMUEL BUTLER

It is recorded of Samuel Butler that on his deathbed he made it plain he wanted to say something and what he wanted to say was that he had written that life was ninety-nine percent chance and he wished to correct this figure to one hundred percent. RUDOLF FLESCH

Chance is the fool's name for fate. FRED ASTAIRE

As much chance as a fart in a hurricane. ANON

Fortune is like the market, where many times, if you can stay a little, the price will fall. FRANCIS BACON

With doubt and dismay you are smitten,
You think there's no chance for you, son?
Why the best books haven't been written,
The best race hasn't been run. BERTON BRALEY

Grab a chance and you won't be sorry for a might-have-been.
ARTHUR RANSOME

Chances rule men and not men chances. HERODOTUS

Most people complain of fortune, few of nature; and the kinder they think the latter has been to them, the more they murmur at what they call the injustice of the former. LORD CHESTERFIELD

Fortune gives too much to many, but to none enough.
MARCUS MARTIAL

Destiny: a tyrant's authority for crime, and a fool's excuse for failure.
AMBROSE BIERCE

As much chance as a celluloid dog chasing an asbestos cat in hell.
ANON

Fortune favors the brave. PUBLIUS TERENCE

What the reason of the ant laboriously drags into a heap, the wind of accident will collect in one breath. FRIEDRICH von SCHILLER

Work and acquire, and thou has chained the wheel of Chance.
RALPH WALDO EMERSON

Chance works for us when we are good captains.
GEORGE MEREDITH

Fortune is ever seen accompanying industry. OLIVER GOLDSMITH

In great affairs we ought to apply ourselves less to creating chances than to profiting from those that offer.
FRANCOIS DUC de la ROCHEFOUCAULD

Affairs sleep soundly when fortune is present. GREEK PROVERB

Fortune does not make men, it only unmasks them.
MADAM RICCOBONI

Depend not on fortune, but on conduct. PUBLILIUS SYRUS

As much chance as a one-legged man in an arse-kicking contest.
ANON

Unless a man has trained himself for his chance, the chance will only make him ridiculous. W. MATTHEWS

What a day may bring, a day may take away. THOMAS FULLER

Every man is the architect of his own future.
GAIUS VALERIUS SALLUST

Fortune slips through one man's grasp to fall, unasked, into another man's lap. EURIPIDES

Chance is the name for our ignorance. LESLIE STEPHEN

Fortune turns everything to the advantage of those she favors.
FRANCOIS DUC de la ROCHEFOUCAULD

Speculation

Speculate but always heed
The best time of the lot
Is when you've got more than you need,
Not need more than you've got.

To speculate in Wall Street when you are not an insider is like buying cows by candlelight. DANIEL DREW

Don't speculate unless you can make it a full-time job. Beware of barbers, beauticians, waiters—of anyone—bringing gifts of "inside" information or "tips." . . . Don't try to buy at the bottom and sell at the top. This can't be done—except by liars. BERNARD M. BARUCH

Dun and Bradstreet will ease the speculation. ANON

There are two times in a man's life when he should not speculate: when he can't afford it, and when he can. MARK TWAIN

I don't think you can spend yourself rich. GEORGE HUMPHREY

Americans sink millions of dollars in unsound financial schemes, one of which is keeping up with the neighbors. HERBERT V. PROCHNOW

One can relish the varied idiocy of human action during a panic to the full, for, while it is a time of great tragedy, nothing is being lost but money. JOHN KENNETH GALBRAITH

To stop speculation, get it in writing. O. A. BATTISTA

Never invest your money in anything that eats or needs repainting.
BILLY ROSE

Wealth is not acquired, as many persons suppose, by fortunate speculations and splendid enterprises, but the daily practice of industry, frugality, and economy. He who relies upon these means will rarely be found destitute, and he who relies upon any other will generally become bankrupt. FRANCIS WAYLAND

He is not fit for riches who is afraid to use them. THOMAS FULLER

Be not penny-wise; riches have wings; sometimes they fly away of themselves, and sometimes they must be set flying to bring in more.
FRANCIS BACON

The successful speculator must be content at times to ignore probably two out of every three apparent opportunities to make money.
CHARLES DOW

Adventure equals risk plus purpose. ROBERT McCLURE

For the merchant, even honesty is a financial speculation.
CHARLES BAUDELAIRE

No amount of speculation takes the place of experience.
CHARLES SANDERS PEIRCE

When speculation has done its worst, two and two still make four.
SAMUEL JOHNSON

People find gold in fields, veins, river beds and pockets. Whichever, it takes work to get it out. ART LINKLETTER

I was raised by a speculator. HARRIET E. B. STOWE

If the world were good for nothing else, it is a fine subject for speculation. WILLIAM HAZLITT

It seems to be a law of American life that whatever enriches us anywhere except in the wallet inevitably becomes uneconomic.
RUSSELL BAKER

Cast thy bread upon the waters:
For thou shalt find it after many days. OLD TESTAMENT

A speculator is a man who observes the future, and acts before it occurs.
BERNARD BARUCH

Almost all rich veins of original and striking speculation have been opened by systematic half-thinkers. JOHN STUART MILL

The practices of good men are more subject to error than their theories and speculations. I will then honor good examples, but I will live by good precepts. ANON

Speculation is the romance of trade, and casts contempt upon all its sober realities It renders the stock-jobber a magician, and the exchange a region of enchantment. WASHINGTON IRVING

The joy and moral stimulation of work no longer must be forgotten in the mad chase of evanescent profits . . . there must be a strict supervision of all the banking and credits and investments; there must be an end to speculation with other people's money. FRANKLIN D. ROOSEVELT

Gambling

When you gamble once again,
It's hard to justify;
You recall both where and when
But can't remember why.

The strength of Monaco is the weakness of the world. H. A. GIBBONS

The gambling known as business looks with austere disfavour upon the business known as gambling. AMBROSE BIERCE

Poker exemplifies the worst aspects of capitalism that have made our country so great. WALTER MATTHAU

Gambling with cards or dice, or stocks, is all one thing; it is getting money without giving an equivalent for it. HENRY WARD BEECHER

Remember this house doesn't beat a player. It merely gives him the chance to beat himself. NICK "THE GREEK" DANDALOS

God does not play dice. ALBERT EINSTEIN

Back of the bar,
in a solo game,
sat Dangerous Dan McGrew,
and watching his luck,
was his light o'love,
the lady that's known as Lou. ROBERT W. SERVICE

If you bet on a horse, that's gambling. If you bet you can make three spades, that's entertainment. If you bet cotton will go up three points, that's business. See the difference? BLACKIE SHERRODE

Insurance: An ingenious modern game of chance in which the player is permitted to enjoy the comfortable conviction that he is beating the man who keeps the table. AMBROSE BIERCE

I backed the right horse, and then the wrong horse went and won. HENRY HERMAN

The odds on hitting the slot machine jackpot are about one in 2,000. ANON

True luck consists not in holding the best of the cards at the table; luckiest he who knows just when to rise and go home. JOHN HAY

There is enough energy wasted in poker to make a hundred thousand successful every year. ARTHUR BRISBANE

Gambling promises the poor what property performs for the rich—something for nothing. GEORGE BERNARD SHAW

The apparent desire to accept the certainty of losing money in the long run in return for the remote possibility of winning it in the short. BERNARD LEVIN

Man is the only animal that plays poker. DON HEROLD

It doesn't say much for society, if gambling is the main method of raising money for good causes. ANON

There is but one good throw upon the dice, which is to throw them away. PAUL CHATFIELD

If you must play, decide upon three things at the start: the rules of the game, the stakes, and the quitting time. CHINESE PROVERB

No dog can go as fast as the money you bet on him. BUD FLANAGAN

Horse racing is a particular interest in that the spectators, who lose money, set many fashions; while the bookmakers, who make money, set none. QUENTIN BELL

He who can predict winning numbers has no need to let off fire-crackers. ERNEST BRAMAH

A poker face is the face that launches a thousand chips. ANON

The better the gambler, the worse the man. PUBLILIUS SYRUS

I'd sooner live among people who cheat at cards than among people who are earnest about not cheating at cards. CLIVE STAPLES LEWIS

It's in gambling that we see the most amazing strokes of luck.
JEAN BAPTISTE MOLIÈRE

Life consists not in holding good cards but in playing those you do hold well. JOSH BILLINGS

Gambling: The sure way of getting nothing for something.
WILSON MIZNER

Gambling is a revolt against boredom. STUART CHASE

The good luck that comes to us in our relations with the industrial world is always the good luck of the gambler—not the glory of the warrior or the reward of the cultivator. ELEMIRE ZOLLA

Gambling: a disease of barbarians superficially civilized.
DEAN WILLIAM R. INGE

Millions of words are written annually purporting to tell how to beat the races, whereas the best possible advice on the subject is found in the three monosyllables, "Do not try." DAN PARKER

Play not for gain, but sport: who plays for more than he can lose with pleasure stakes his heart. GEORGE HERBERT

A gambler is nothing but a man who makes his living out of hope.
WILLIAM BOLITHO

Man is a gaming animal. He must be always trying to get the better in something or other. CHARLES LAMB

Every one knows that horse-racing is carried on mainly for the delight and profit of fools, ruffians, and thieves. GEORGE GISSING

Nine gamblers could not feed a single rooster. YUGOSLAV PROVERB

One throw of the dice will never abolish chance.
STEPHANE MALLARME

Remember that time is an avid gambler who has no need to cheat to win every time. That's the law! CHARLES BAUDELAIRE

I must complain the cards are ill-shuffled till I have a good hand. JOHATHAN SWIFT

If you won't gamble enough to hurt you, it won't do you any good to win. BILL LEAR

Gaming is the son of avarice, and the father of despair. FRENCH PROVERB

Gambling is the child of avarice, but the parent of prodigality. CHARLES CALEB COLTON

Gambling is the child of avarice, the brother of iniquity, and the father of mischief. GEORGE WASHINGTON

Gambling is a kind of tacit confession that those engaged therein do, in general, exceed the bounds of their respective fortunes; and therefore they cast lots to determine on whom the ruin shall at present fall, that the rest may be saved a little longer. SIR WILLIAM BLACKSTONE

The urge to gamble is so universal and its practice so pleasurable that I assume it must be civil. HEYWOOD HALE BROUN

I think the primary motive in back of most gambling is the excitement of it While gamblers naturally want to win, the majority of them derive pleasure even if they lose. The desire to win, rather than the excitement invovled, seems to me to be the compelling force behind speculation. JOE KENNEDY

Security

Make often a call.
To check if it's wrong,
For nothing at all
Is secure for long.

There is no such thing as security. There never has been. GERMAINE GREER

Businessmen tend to grow old early. They are committed to security and stability. They won't rock the boat and won't gamble, denying the future for a near-sighted present. They forget what made them successful in the first place. PETER C. GOLDMARK

Who is to guard the guards themselves? DECIMUS JUVENAL

Buy gold, silver, Swiss francs and a gun. HARRY BROWNE

If money is your only hope for independence, you will never have it. The only real security that a man can have in this world is a reserve of knowledge, experience and ability. HENRY FORD

Get double security from your relatives. EDGAR WATSON HOWE

The 1976 Olympics could no more lose money than I could have a baby.
MAYOR of MONTREAL

There was an old man of Nantucket
Who kept all his cash in a bucket;
But his daughter named Nan,
Ran away with a man—
And as for the bucket, Nantucket. ANON

New York is the insecurity center of America.
JOHN WEITZ and EVERETT MAHLIN

The way to be safe is never to be secure. PROVERB

A reasonable probability is the only certainty.
EDGAR WATSON HOWE

I like terra firma—the more firma, the less terra.
GEORGE S. KAUFMAN

There is no security on this earth. There is only opportunity.
GENERAL DOUGLAS MacARTHUR

The best lightning-rod for your protection is your own spine.
RALPH WALDO EMERSON

Security depends not so much upon how much you have, as upon how much you can do without. And that is true for society as well as for the individual. JOSEPH WOOD KRUTCH

Only the insecure strive for security. WAYNE DYER

I knew one thing: as soon as anyone said you didn't need a gun, you'd better take one along that worked. RAYMOND CHANDLER

Authorized personnel only. If you had to ask, you aren't. KEN MAUZY

We spend our time searching for security, and hate it when we get it. JOHN STEINBECK

A lock is meant only for honest men. YIDDISH PROVERB

Security is an invitation to indolence. ROD McKUEN

The man who looks for security, even in the mind, is like a man who would chop off his limbs in order to have artificial ones which will give him no pain or trouble. HENRY MILLER

You can take better care of your secret than another can. RALPH WALDO EMERSON

The protected man doesn't need luck; therefore, it seldom visits him. ALAN HARRINGTON

Most people want security in this world, not liberty. HENRY LOUIS MENCKEN

It is folly to bolt the door with a boiled carrot. ENGLISH PROVERB

To keep oneself safe does not mean to bury oneself. LUCIUS ANNAEUS SENECA

The superior man, when resting in safety, does not forget that danger may come. When in a state of security he does not forget the possibility of ruin. When all is orderly, he does not forget that disaster may come. Thus his person is not endangered, and his States and all their clans are preserved. CONFUCIUS

Only these means of security are good, are certain, are lasting, that depend on yourself and your own vigor. NICCOLO MACHIAVELLI

That which everybody guards will soon disappear. POLISH PROVERB

It is always the secure who are humble.
GILBERT KEITH CHESTERTON

He who is surety is never sure of himself. Take advice, and never be security for more than you are quite willing to lose. Remember the word of the wise man: "He that is surety for a stranger shall smrt for it; and he that hateth suretyship is sure." CHARLES HADDON SPURGEON

Only in growth, reform and chance, paradoxically enough, is true security to be found. ANNE MORROW LINDBERG

Uncertainty and expectation are the joys of life. Security is an insipid thing, and the overtaking and possessing of a wish, discovers the folly of the chase. WILLIAM CONGREVE

Prudence

There's a helluva lot to be said
For the ordinary pin. Hurrah!
It's dead straight and it's head
Stops it from going too far.

The amount of prudence and sagacity needful for the successive transaction of business depends comparatively little on the scale of operation. Sometimes, indeed, the larger the scale the easier the task.
SIR HENRY TAYLOR

An ounce of prudence is worth a pound of gold. TOBIAS SMOLLETT

A prudent person profits from personal experience, a wise one from the experience of others. DR. JOSEPH COLLINS

A man who raises himself by degrees to wealth and power, contracts, in the course of this protracted labor, habits of prudence and restraint which he cannot afterwards shake off. A man cannot gradually enlarge his mind as he does his house. ALEXIS de TOCQUEVILLE

No call alligator long mouth till you pass him. JAMAICAN PROVERB

My advice to you, if you should ever be in a hold-up, is to line up with the cowards and save your bravery for an occasion when it may be of some benefit to you. O. HENRY

There is nothing more imprudent than excessive prudence.
CHARLES CALEB COLTON

When you have nothing to say, or to hide, there is no need to be prudent
ANDRE GIDÉ

Moderation, after all, is only the belief that you will be a better man tomorrow than you were yesterday. MURRAY KEMPTON

Be moderate in prosperity, prudent in adversity. PERIANDER

Chance usually favours the prudent man. JOSEPH JOUBERT

Some people are making such thorough preparation for rainy days that they aren't enjoying today's sunshine. WILLIAM FEATHER

I've got money so I'm a Conservative. LORD THOMSON of FLEET

Never depend on anyone except yourself! JEAN de la FONTAINE

I have lived in this world just long enough to look carefully the second time into things that I am most certain of the first time.
JOSH BILLINGS

Let sleeping dogs lie. ENGLISH PROVERB

Chance fights ever on the side of the prudent. EURIPIDES

The better part of valour is discretion. WILLIAM SHAKESPEARE

None are rash when they are not seen by anybody.
LESZINSKI STANISLAUS

That man is prudent who neither hopes nor fears anything from the uncertain events of the future. ANATOLE FRANCE

Prudence is a rich, ugly old maid courted by incapacity.
WILLIAM BLAKE

A prudent man does not make the goat his gardener.
HUNGARIAN PROVERB

Prudence consists in the power to recognize the nature of disadvantages and to take the less disagreeable as good. NICCOLO MACHIAVELLI

Never draw your dirk when a blow will do it. SCOTTISH PROVERB

Prudence is of more frequent use than any other intellectual quality; it is exerted on slight occasions, and called into act by the cursory business of common life. SAMUEL JOHNSON

So soon as prudene has begun to grow up in the brain, like a dismal fungus, it finds its first expression in a paralysis of generous acts.
ROBERT LOUIS STEVENSON

No other protection is wanting, provided you are under the guidance of prudence. JUVENAL

Nothing can be done at once hastily and prudently.
PUBLILIUS SYRUS

If the search for riches were sure to be successful, though I should become a groom, with a whip in my hand to get them, I will do so. As the search may not be successful, I will follow after that which I love.
CONFUCIUS

When defeat is inevitable, it is wisest to yield.
MARCUS FABIUS QUINTILIANUS

Prudence is sometimes stretched too far, until it blocks the road of progress. TEHYI HSIEH

Nothing more unqualifies a man to act with prudence than a misfortune that is attended with shame and guilt. JONATHAN SWIFT

The prudence of the best heads is often defeated by the tenderness of the best of hearts. HENRY FIELDING

I consider it a mark of great prudence in a man to abstain from threats or any contemptuous expressions, for neither of these weaken the enemy, but the one makes him more cautious, and the other excites his hatred, and a desire to revenge himself NICCOLO MACHIAVELLI

Prudence operates on life in the same manner as rules on composition: it produces vigilance rather than elevation, rather prevents loss than procures advantage; and often escapes miscarriages, but seldom reaches either power or honor. . . . Prudence keeps life safe, but does not often make it happy. SAMUEL JOHNSON

Optimism

An optimist is often wrong
But he gets a lot more done.
His worries don't last all that long
And he has a lot more fun.

Being optimistic after you've got everything you want don't count.
FRANK McKINNEY HUBBARD

An optimist is one who doesn't care what happens, as long as it doesn't happen to him. CURT BOIS

An optimist is merely an ex-pessimist with his pockets full of money, his digestion in good condition, and his wife in the country.
HELEN ROWLAND

Optimism is making the most of all that comes and least of all that goes.
ANON

The most optimistic person I ever met was undoubtedly a young artist in Paris who, without a franc in his pocket, went into a swanky restaurant and ate a dozen oysters in the hope of finding a pearl to pay the bill.
SACHA GUITRY

I could rather be an optimist and be right 50 per cent of the time than a pessimist and be right all of the time. O. A. BATTISTA

Optimism is a kind of heart stimulant—the digitalis of failure.
ELBERT HUBBARD

I am an optimist. It does not seem too much use being anything else.
SIR WINSTON CHURCHILL

An optimist talks about what a fool he used to be. BUDDY SATZ

A pessimist forgets to laugh, but an optimist laughs to forget.
HENRY V. PROCHNOW

In these times you have to be an optimist to open your eyes when you wake in the morning. CARL SANDBURG

An optimist tells you to cheer up when things are going his way.
EDWARD R. MURROW

When people are happy, optimists are out of a job. AGNES REPPLIER

I am not an optimist, I am a possibilist. JULIAN HUXLEY

Our notion of an optimist is a man who, knowing that each year was worse than the preceding, thinks next year will be better, and a pessimist is a man who kows the next year can't be any worse than the last one. FRANKLIN P. ADAMS

Optimism: The noble temptation to see too much in everything.
GILBERT KEITH CHESTERTON

An optimist is a guy who never had much experience.
DONALD ROBERT PERRY MARQUIS

The average pencil is seven inches long, with just a half-inch rubber—in case you thought optimism was dead. *Los Angeles Times Syndicate*

An optimist is a fellow who believes what's going to be will be postponed. FRANK McKINNEY HUBBARD

Optimism is believing that what will come, and must come, shall come well. EDWIN ARNOLD

The latest definition of an optimist is one who fills up his crossword puzzle in ink. CLEMENT SHORTER

There is no sadder sight than a young pessimist, except an old optimist.
MARK TWAIN

An optimist is a fellow who believes a housefly is looking for a way to get out. GEORGE JEAN NATHAN

Optimism approves of everything, submits to everything, believes everything; it is the virtue above all of the taxpayer. GEORGES BERNANOS

Optimist: the sort of man who marries his sister's best friend.
HENRY LOUIS MENCKEN

Optimists do not wait for improvement; they achieve it.
PAUL von KEPPLER

An optimist can always see the bright side of the other fellow's misfortune. *Richmond News-Leader*

To the question whether I am a pessimist or an optimist, I answer that my knowledge is pessimistic, but my willing and hoping are optimistic.
ALBERT SCHWEITZER

Optimism is the mania of maintaining that everything is right when it is wrong. FRANCOIS VOLTAIRE

Optimism: The doctrine or belief that everything is beautiful, including what is ugly, everything good, especially the bad, and everything right that is wrong. AMBROSE BIERCE

What passes for optimism is most often the effect of an intellectual error.
RAYMOND ARON

Circumstances break men's bones; it has never been shown that they break men's optimism. GILBERT KEITH CHESTERTON

Optimism and self-pity are the positive and negative poles of modern cowardice. CYRIL CONNOLLY

Optimism is the content of small men in high places.
F. SCOTT FITZGERALD

Learn to be pleased with everything; with wealth, so far as it makes us beneficial to others; with poverty, for not having much to care for; and with obscurity, for being unenvied. PLUTARCH

Some people are always grumbling that roses have thorns; I am thankful that thorns have roses. ALPHONSE KARR

I have the Pollyana pest
who says that All is for the Best. FRANKLIN P. ADAMS

If you pretend to be good, the world takes you very seriously. If you pretend to be bad, it doesn't. Such is the astounding stupidity of optimism.
OSCAR WILDE

The essence of optimism is that it takes no account of the present, but it is a source of inspiration, of vitality and hope where others have resigned, it enables a man to hold his head high, to claim the future for himself and not to abandon it to his enemy.
DIETRICH BONHOEFFER

Pessimism

A pessimist is always cursed,
As you might have guessed,
To make results become the worst
Out of his very best.

There have always been many pessimists whenever there have been many people whose income has diminished. BERTRAND RUSSELL

A pessimist is one who, of two evils, picks them both. ANON

Pessimism is a luxury that a Jew never can allow himself.
GOLDA MEIR

Ninety per cent of everything is crap. THEODORE STURGEON

When things appear to be improving,
you must have overlooked something. ANON

A pessimist is one who has been intimately acquainted with an optimist.
ELBERT HUBBARD

If you keep saying things are going to be bad you have a good chance of being a prophet. ISAAC BASHEVIS SINGER

A pessimist is one who feels bad when he feels good, for fear he'll feel worse when he feels better.
ANON

A pessimist is tied in nots.
DINAH BROWN

A Pessimist is one who makes difficulties of his opportunities; an optimist is one who makes opportunities of his difficulties
REGINALD B. MANSELL

A pessimist is one who builds dungeons in the air.
WALTER WINCHELL

The man who is a pessimist before forty-eight knows too much; if he is an optimist after it, he knows too little.
MARK TWAIN

The optimist sees the doughnut,
The pessimist, the hole.
McLANDBURGH WILSON

If it weren't for the optimist, the pessimist would never know how happy he wasn't.
ANON

The optimist proclaims that we live in the best of all possible worlds, and the pessimist fears this is true.
JAMES BRANCH CABELL

A pessimist is a person who has had to listen to too many optimists.
DONALD ROBERT PERRY MARQUIS

Pessimist: one who sizes himself up and gets sore about it.
EDMUND FULLER

A pessimist is a man who thinks everybody is as nasty as himself, and hates them for it.
GEORGE BERNARD SHAW

Only the man who finds everything wrong and expects it to get worse is thought to have a clear brain.
JOHN KENNETH GALBRAITH

Show me a person with plenty of worries and troubles and I will show you a person who, whatever he is, is not a pessimist.
GILBERT KEITH CHESTERTON

The pessimist is the man who believes things couldn't possibly be worse, to which the optimist replies, "Oh, yes, they could."
VLADIMIR BUKOVSKY

Much pessimism is caused by ascribing to others the feelings you would feel if you were in their place. WILLIAM SOMERSET MAUGHAM

There are moments when everything goes well; don't be frightened, it won't last. JULES RENARD

Pessimism does win us great happy moments. MAX BEERBOHM

Pessimism is the only name that men of weak nerves give to wisdom. BERNARDO DE VOTO

A pessimist is a person who stops by the meat market before he goes hunting and has a chicken sent home. ANON

We used to say that things will get worse before they get better; now we say they will be worse before they're still worse
PROFESSOR ROBERT TRIFFIN

My pessimism goes to the point of suspecting the sincerity of the pessimists JEAN ROSTAND

No man should think himself a zero and think he can do nothing about the state of the world. BERNARD M. BARUCH

Pessimism is the one ism which kills the soul. JOHN BUCHAN

It is not usually our ideas that make us optimists or pessimists, but it is our optimism or our pessimism, of physiological or perhaps pathological origin, as much the one as the other, that makes our ideas.
MIGUEL de UNAMUNO

To a profound pessimist about life, being in danger is not depressing.
F. SCOTT FITZGERALD

A pessimist sees only the dark side of the clouds, and mopes; a philosopher sees both sides, and shrugs; an optimist doesn't see the clouds at all—he's walking on them. D. O. FLYNN

Scratch a pessimist, and you find often a defender of privilege.
LORD BEVERIDGE

VIII ATTITUDES

Ruthlessness

The very ruthless
Are sometimes toothless.

A thick skin is a gift from God. KONRAD ADENAUER

To be a great autocrat you must be a great barbarian.
JOSEPH CONRAD

He wouldn't give a duck a drink if he owned Lake Michigan. ANON

You have to be a bastard to make it, and that's a fact. And the Beatles are the biggest bastards on earth. JOHN LENNON

Succeed we must, at all cost—even if it means being a dead millionaire at fifty. LOUIS KRONENBERGER

If you're strong enough, there are no precedents.
F. SCOTT FITZGERALD

Nothing is ever accomplished by a reasonable man.
GEORGE BERNARD SHAW

Scared cows make great hamburgers. ROBERT REISNER

He would skin a flint. JOHN BERTHELSON

This is the Law of the Yukon, that only the strong shall thrive. That surely the weak shall perish, and only the Fit survive.
ROBERT WILLIAM SERVICE

You cannot shake hands with a clenched fist. INDIRA GANDHI

"There's been an accident," they said,
"Your servant's cut in half; he's dead!"
"Indeed!" said Mr. Jones, "and please,
Send me the half that's got my keys." HARRY GRAHAM

Constant exposure to dangers will breed contempt for them. SENECA

The public be damned! WILLIAM HENRY VANDERBILT

You are going to let me do what you want done in the way that I want to do it. SIR DONALD WOLFIT

I'm sorry I missed. SQUEAKY FROMME

If any demonstrator ever lays down in front of my car, it'll be the last car he'll ever lay down in front of. GEORGE WALLACE

Frankly, my dear, I don't give a damn. CLARK GABLE

Action, swiftness, violence, power: these are native, homegrown American qualities, derived from the vast continent that has been ours to open up, and the big prizes that have made our economy into a jungle where the law is eat or be eaten. MAX LERNER

We will either find a way, or make one. HANNIBAL

We should go in and win—or else get out. RUSSELL LONG

Give the investigators an hors d'oeuvre and maybe they won't come back for the main course. RICHARD NIXON

The one important thing in life is to see to it that you are never beaten.
ANDRÉ MALRAUX

How you play the game is for college boys. When you're playing for money, winning is the only thing that matters. LEO DUROCHER

Damn the consequences. LORD MILNER

I am in the habit of shooting from time to time, and if I sometimes make mistakes, at least I have shot. HERMANN GÖRING

I have not yet begun to fight. JOHN PAUL JONES

I don't care what anybody says. I'm to do exactly what I want to do. If it's illegal, immoral, or fattening, Adam Powell is going to do it. I intend to live my life. ADAM CLAYTON POWELL

I bomb, therefore I am. PHILIP SLATER

When you have to kill a man it costs nothing to be polite.
WINSTON CHURCHILL

Presidents in general are not lovable, they've had to do too much to get where they are. WALTER LIPPMAN

The American beauty rose can be produced in all its splendor only by sacrificing the early buds that grow up around it.
JOHN D. ROCKEFELLER

If an injury has to be done to a man it should be so severe that his vengeance need not be feared. NICCOLO MACHIAVELLI

A vain man can never be utterly ruthless: he wants to win applause and therefore he accommodates himself to others.
JOHANN WOLFGANG von GOETHE

Trust

Trust not
The person
Who trusts not.

Put not your trust in money, but put your money in trust.
OLIVER WENDELL HOLMES

In God we trust; all others must pay cash. AMERICAN PROVERB

I trust no one, not even myself. JOSEPH STALIN

Better to trust the man who is frequently in error than the one who is never in doubt. ERIC SEVAREID

There is trust even among thieves. LATIN PROVERB

The man who trusts men will make fewer mistakes than the man who distrusts them. COUNT CAVOUR

Trust one who has proved it. PUBLIUS VIRGIL

When a man has no reason to trust himself, he trusts in luck. EDGAR WATSON HOWE

Trust diminishes as power increases. ANON

Put your trust in God, my boys, and keep your powder dry. VALENTINE BLACKER

Never trust any superior who always finds fault with his inferior, nor any inferior who never finds fault with his superior. ANON

It is better to suffer wrong than to do it, and happier to be sometimes cheated than not to trust. SAMUEL JOHNSON

I think that we may safely trust a good deal more than we do. HENRY DAVID THOREAU

Trust him little who praises all, him less who censures all, and him least who is indifferent about all. JOHN CASPAR LAVATER

If you trust before you try,
You may repent before you die. RANDOLPH RAY

One must be fond of people and trust them if one is not to make a mess of life. EDWARD MORGAN FORSTER

I wonder men dare trust themselves with men. WILLIAM SHAKESPEARE

To be trusted is a greater compliment than to be loved. GEORGE MACDONALD

Trust only those who have the courage to contradict you with respect, and who value your character more than your favor. FRANCIOS de FENELON

You may be deceived if you trust too much, but you will live in torment if you do not trust enough. FRANK CRANE

The vanity of being known to be trusted with a secret is generally one of the chief motives to disclose it. SAMUEL JOHNSON

Men trust rather to their eyes than to their ears. The effect of precepts is, therefore, slow and tedious, while that of examples is summary and effectual. LUCIUS ANNAEUS SENECA

When a secret is revealed, it is the fault of the man who has intrusted it.
JEAN de la BRUYÈRE

It is much more difficult than you can imagine to find a heart that is truly to be trusted. GIAM BATTISTA CINTHIO GIRALDI

Do not trust all men, but trust men of worth; the former course is silly, the latter a mark of prudence. DEMOCRITUS

No men living are more worthy to be trusted than those who toil up from poverty, none less inclined to take or touch aught which they have not honestly earned. Let them beware of surrendering a political power which they already possess and which, if surrendered, will surely be used to close the door of advancement against such as they and to fix new disabilities and burdens upon them till all of liberty shall be lost
ABRAHAM LINCOLN

Suspicion

You may be right or may be wrong
And it can cause some laughter;
You will learn before too long
But cannot tell till after.

Where large sums of money are concerned, it is advisable to trust nobody. AGATHA CHRISTIE

If you suspect a man, don't employ him, and if you employ him, don't suspect him CHINESE PROVERB

Our distrust is very expensive. RALPH WALDO EMERSON

The less we know the more we suspect. JOSH BILLINGS

Suspicion begets suspicion. PUBLILIUS SYRUS

The always suspicious
Are the most pernicious. ANON

Let us not look back in anger of forward in fear, but around in awareness. JAMES THURBER

Trust in God, but tie your camel. PERSIAN PROVERB

Trust everybody, but cut the cards. FINLEY PETER DUNNE

Never trust a man with short legs; brains too near their bottoms. NOEL COWARD

Suspicion on one side breeds suspicion on the other. JOHN F. KENNEDY

He gradually wormed his way out of my confidence. NUNNALLY JOHNSON

The chief lesson I have learned in a long life is that the only way to make a man trustworthy is to trust him, and the surest way to make him untrustworthy is to distrust him and show your distrust. HENRY L. STIMSON

There is no rule more invariable than that we are paid for our suspicions by finding what we suspected. HENRY DAVID THOREAU

Always mistrust a subordinate who never finds fault with his superior. JOHN CHURTON COLLINS

Never trust a man whose eyes are too close to his nose. LYNDON B. JOHNSON

There is nothing makes a man suspect much, more than to know little. FRANCIS BACON

We have to distrust each other. It is our only defense against betrayal. TENNESSEE WILLIAMS

The over-suspicious are fooled most often. ANON

We are always paid for our suspicions by finding what we suspect.
HENRY DAVID THOREAU

Anyone who has bad luck always seems to get suspicious and to take offense at the slightest thing. PUBLIUS TERENCE

Never suspect people. It's better to be deceived or mistaken, which is only human, after all, than to be suspicious, which is common.
STARK YOUNG

Open suspecting of others comes of secretly condemning ourselves.
SIR PHILIP SIDNEY

Ignorance is the mother of suspicion. WILLIAM R. ALGER

Trust the friends of today as if they will be enemies tomorrow.
BALTASAR GRACIAN

Self-respect: the secure feeling that no one, as yet, is suspicious.
HENRY LOUIS MENCKEN

It is a matter of regret that many low, mean, suspicions turn out to be well founded. EDGAR WATSON HOWE

Always to think the worst, I have ever found to be the mark of a mean spirit and a base soul. LORD BOLINGBROKE

Suspicion is a thing very few people can entertain without letting the hypothesis turn, in their minds, into fact. DAVID CORT

He who is too much afraid of being duped has lost the power of being magnanimous. HENRI FREDERIC AMIEL

If you would avoid suspicion, do not lace your shoes in a melon field.
CHINESE PROVERB

You may be deceived if you trust too much, but you will live in torment if you do not trust enough. FRANK CRANE

You risk just as much in being credulous as in being suspicious.
DENIS DIDEROT

To be suspicious is to invite treachery. FRANCOIS VOLTAIRE

When you grow suspicious of a person and begin a system of espionage upon him, your punishment will be that you will find your suspicions true. ELBERT HUBBARD

Suspicion is rather a virtue than a fault, as long as it does like a dog that watches and does not bite. LORD HALIFAX

Distrust all those who love you extremely upon a very slight acquaintance and without any visible reason. EARL of CHESTERFIELD

Never trust the man who hath reason to suspect that you know he hath injured you. HENRY FIELDING

There is nothing makes a man suspect much, more than to know little, and therefore men should remedy suspicion by procuring to know more, and not keep their suspicions in smother. FRANCIS BACON

Hope

If you check on the predictions
That were in your horoscope,
More frequent are the frictions
Than the things for which you hope.

Hope is the poor man's income. DANISH PROVERB

Hope: a pathological belief in the occurrence of the impossible.
HENRY LOUIS MENCKEN

Life for Americans is always becoming, never being.
ALBERT EINSTEIN

America is a nation with many flaws, but hopes so vast that only the cowardly would refuse to acknowledge them. JAMES MICHENER

Hope is the feeling you have that the feeling you have isn't permanent.
JEAN KERR

The hope that springs eternal
Springs right up your behind. IAN DRURY

If you ever find happiness by hunting for it, you will find it as the old woman did her spectacles—safe on her nose all the time.
JOSH BILLINGS

Hope is like the wag of a dog's tail when he is waiting for a bone.
ANON

Hope deceives more men than cunning does.
MARQUIS de VAUVENARGUES

There is nothing so well known as that we should not expect something for nothing—but we all do and call it Hope. EDGAR WATSON HOWE

Never grow a wishbone, daughter, where your backbone ought to be.
CLEMENTINE PADDLEFORD

Do not invest your whole life in one hope. AUSTON O'MALLEY

While there's tea there's hope. SIR ARTHUR WING PINERO

Hope . . . suggests that every conclusion unfavorable to oneself must be an error of the mind. PAUL VALERY

Hope is a commodity none of us ever runs out of. But you've got to hope reasonably. JOHN PETER

Hope is a risk that must be run. GEORGES BERNANOS

The maximum danger implies the maximum hope. ALBERT CAMUS

Hope—fortune's cheating lottery, where for one prize, a hundred blanks there be. ABRAHAM COWLEY

Hope is the only thing that is not taxed today. LORD BIRKENHEAD

Pray: v: to ask that the laws of the universe be annulled in behalf of a single petitioner confessedly unworthy. AMBROSE BIERCE

My motto is: Contented with little, yet wishing for more.
CHARLES LAMB

I never knew a man who lived on hope but what spent his old age at somebody else's expense. JOSH BILLINGS

To have his path made clear for him is the aspiration of every human being in our beclouded and tempestuous existence. JOSEPH CONRAD

The significance of a man is not in what he attains but rather in what he longs to attain. KAHLIL GIBRAN

Hope is a prodigal young heir, and experience is his banker, but his drafts are seldom honored since there is often a heavy balance against him, because he draws largely on a small capital and is not yet in possession. CHARLES CALEB COLTON

In general, when we are looking forward to something, the shorter the time is the longer it seems to us—because we measure it in shorter units or simply because we think of measuring it. MARCEL PROUST

Hope is the only universal liar who never loses his reputation for veracity. ROBERT G. INGERSOLL

Before we set our hearts too much upon any thing, let us examine how happy those are who already possess it.

FRANCOIS DUC de la ROCHEFOUCAULD

In life, as in whist, hope nothing from the way cards may be dealt to you. Play the cards whatever they be, to the best of your skill.

EDWARD GEORGE BULWER-LYTTON

If it were not for hopes, the heart would break. THOMAS FULLER

We do not succeed in changing things according to our desire but gradually our desires change. MARCEL PROUST

No man is happy without a delusion of some kind. Delusions are as necessary to our happiness as realities. CHRISTIAN NESTELL BOVEE

We grow great by dreams. All big men are dreamers. They see things in the soft haze of a spring day or in the red fire of a long winter's evening. Some of us let these great dreams die, but others nourish and protect them, nurse them through bad days till they bring them to the sunshine and light which comes always to those who sincerely hope that their dreams will come true. WOODROW WILSON

Keep your face to the sunshine and you cannot see the shadow.

HELEN KELLER

The man who will live above his present circumstances is in great danger of soon living much beneath them; or as the Italian proverb says, "The man that lives by hope, will die by despair." JOSEPH ADDISON

Extreme hopes are born of extreme misery. BERTRAND RUSSELL

Superstition is the religion of feeble minds. EDMUND BURKE

Of all the forces that make for a better world, none is so indispensable, none so powerful, as hope. Without hope men are only half alive. With hope they think and dream and work. CHARLES SAWYER

Cut the wings of your hopes and hens lest they lead you a weary dance after them. BENJAMIN FRANKLIN

A curse on every wish that blurs the sight, paralyzes the tongue, cramps the hand, and prevents the truth being seen, said and written.
THEODOR HAECKER

If you prefer illusions to realities, it is only because all decent realities have eluded you and left you in the lurch, or else your contempt for the world is mere hypocrisy and funk. GEORGE SANTAYANA

He that hopes no good fears no ill. THOMAS FULLER

Hopes are but the dreams of those who are awake. PINDAR

In all things it is better to hope than to despair.
JOHANN WOLFGANG von GOETHE

Confidence

You're only once upon this earth,
You cannot visit twice;
If you do not yet know your worth,
No one will raise your price.

A man cannot be comfortable without his own approval.
MARK TWAIN

Confidence is that assured feeling you get just before you fall flat on your face. ANON

No one can make you feel inferior without your consent. ELEANOR ROOSEVELT

You invite more trouble by underrating yourself than by overrating yourself. ANON

I am one of those who would rather sink with faith than swim without it. STANLEY BALDWIN

I am as my Creator made me, and since He is satisfied, so am I. MINNIE SMITH

A man has the right to toot his own horn to his heart's content, so long as he stays in his own home, keeps his windows closed and does not make himself obnoxious to his neighbors. TIORIO

Confidence: the feeling that makes one believe a man, even when one knows that one would lie in his place. HENRY LOUIS MENCKEN

Confidence in another's integrity is no slight evidence of one's own. MICHEL de MONTAIGNE

He who undervalues himself is justly undervalued by others. WILLIAM HAZLITT

Confidence is that feeling you have before you know better. ANON

A superiority complex quite often outlives the condition that brought it into existence. ARTHUR STRINGER

He who knows his incapacity knows something. MARGEURITE de VALOIS

Confidence contributes more to conversation than wit. FRANCOIS DUC de la ROCHEFOUCAULD

If you do not believe in yourself, do not blame others for lacking faith in you. BRENDAN FRANCIS

The shy man usually finds that he has been shy without cause, and that, in practice, no one takes the slightest notice of him. ROBERT LYND

The trouble with the world is that the stupid are cocksure and the intelligent full of doubt. BERTRAND RUSSELL

If I cannot brag of knowing something, then I brag of not knowing it, at any rate brag. RALPH WALDO EMERSON

Your chaps are either positive that they are always right about everything or positive that they are always wrong. Neither attitude inspires much confidence. ANON

No one who deserves confidence ever solicits it. CHURTON COLLINS

I have great faith in fools; self-confidence my friends call it. EDGAR ALLAN POE

Confidence goeth farther in company than good sense. EDMUND FULLER

For a man to achieve all that is demanded of him he must regard himself as greater than he is. JOHANN WOLFGANG von GOETHE

I'm so glad I never feel important, it does complicate life. ELEANOR ROOSEVELT

Danger breeds best on too much confidence. PIERRE CORNEILLE

Confidence always gives pleasure to the man in whom it is placed. FRANCOIS DUC de la ROCHEFOUCAULD

The most delightful surprise in life is to suddenly recognize your own worth. MAXWELL MALTZ

Attempt easy tasks as if they were difficult, and difficult as if they were easy; in the one case that confidence may not fall asleep, in the other that it may not be dismayed. BALTASAR GRACIAN

Confidence is the only bond of friendship. PUBLILIUS SYRUS

Jimmy taught me a long time ago that you do the best you can and don't worry about the criticisms. Once you accept the fact that you're not perfect, then you develop some confidence. ROSALYNN CARTER

It's fine to believe in ourselves but we mustn't be too easily convinced. BURTON WILLIS

Loyalty is inspired by confidence and that confidence hinges on truth.
E. J. THOMAS

There is not one wise man in twenty that will praise himself.
WILLIAM SHAKESPEARE

A man is a kind of inverted thermometer, the bulb uppermost and the column of self-evaluation is all the time going up and down.
OLIVER WENDELL HOLMES

It is just as damaging to think you are superior as it is to think you are inferior. People who think they are superior often find it difficult, if not impossible, to learn from others or to profit from their own mistakes.
ALLEN FAY

The confidence which we have in ourselves engenders the greatest part of that we have in others. FRANCOIS DUC de la ROCHEFOUCAULD

Let him that thinketh he standeth take heed in case he fall. *Corinthians*

It is native personality, and that alone, that endows a man to stand before presidents or generals, or in any distinguished collection, with aplomb—and not culture, or any intellect whatever.
WALT WHITMAN

A man can believe in all the gods and goddesses that ever existed, but if he does not have faith in himself, his faith is useless.
SWAMI VIVEKANANDA

'Umble we are, 'umble we have been, 'umble we shall ever be.
CHARLES DICKENS

Every man who attacks my belief diminishes in some degree my confidence in it, and therefore makes me uneasy, and I am angry with him who makes me uneasy. SAMUEL JOHNSON

It is wonderful how soon men acquire talents for offices of trust and importance. The higher the situation, the higher the opinion it gives us of ourselves, and as is our confidence, so is our capacity. We assume an equality with circumstance. WILLIAM HAZLITT

There are admirable potentialities in every human being. Believe in your strength and your youth. Learn to repeat endlessly to yourself, "It all depends on me." ANDRE GALE

Perfection

All the while, I'm
In the top section,
Let others waste time,
Seeking perfection.

I am easily satisfied with the very best. WINSTON CHURCHILL

A diamond with a flaw is better than a common stone that is perfect.
CHINESE PROVERB

The sad truth is that excellence makes people nervous.
SHANA ALEXANDER

Perfection has one grave defect. It is apt to be dull.
WILLIAM SOMERSET MAUGHAM

When a man says that he is perfect already, there is only one of two places for him, and that is heaven or the lunatic asylum.
HENRY WARD BEECHER

Of what small spots pure white complains. JOHN DONNE

Have no fear of perfection—you'll never reach it. SALVADOR DALI

All my life I've always had the urge to do things better than anybody else. Even in school, if it was something like making up a current events booklet, I'd want mine to be the best in the class.
BABE DIDRIKSON ZAHARIAS

The idea of perfection always gives one a chance to talk without knowing facts. AGNES SLIGH TURNBULL

In anything at all, perfection is finally attained not when there is no longer anything to add, but when there is no longer anything to take.
ANTOINE de SAINT-EXUPERY

I'm not hard to work with. I just like things done my way.
GEORGE J. HECHT

Nobody's perfect. JOE E. LEWIS

It is a funny thing about life; if you refuse to accept anything but the best you very often get it. SOMERSET MAUGHAM

If you want things to be right you have to do them yourself. JACQUELINE ONASSIS

Total freedom from error is what none of us will allow to our neighbours; however, we may be inclined to flirt a little with such spotless perfection. CHARLES CALEB COLTON

The maxim "Nothing avails but perfection" may be spelled "Paralysis." SIR WINSTON CHURCHILL

We doubt that we could live with a clock that was always right any more than with a person who was always right. ELWYN BROOKS WHITE

Perfection is no more a requisite to art than to heroes. Frigidaires are perfect. Beauty limps. My frigidaire has had to be replaced. NED ROREM

Everything superlatively good has always been quantitatively small, and scarce. BALTASAR GRACIAN

It is necessary to try to surpass oneself always; this occupation ought to last as long as life. CHRISTINA, QUEEN of SWEDEN

Trifles make perfection, and perfection is no trifle. MICHELANGELO

When a man is no longer anxious to do better than well, he is done for. ALBERT EUSTACE HAYDON

If you expect perfection from people, your whole life is a series of disappointments, grumblings, and complaints. If, on the contrary, you pitch your expectations low, taking folks as the inefficient creatures which they are, you are frequently surprised by having them perform better than you had hoped. BRUCE BARTON

You better do the right thing. JIMMY "THE WEASEL" FRATIANNO

A man must be strong enough to mold the peculiarity of his imperfections into the perfection of his peculiarities. WALTER RATHENUA

The indefatigable pursuit of an unattainable perfection even though it consists in nothing more than in the pounding of an old piano, is what alone gives a meaning to our lives on the unavailing star.

LOGAN PEARSALL SMITH

It is folly to expect men to do all that they may reasonably be expected to do.

RICHARD WHATELY

The activist cannot be a perfectionist. He's got to be a realist. And he ought to be an idealist.

EDMUND MUSKIE

True perfection is achieved only by those who are prepared to destroy it. It is a by-product of greatness.

LORD KENNETH CLARK

We find fault with perfection itself.

BLAISE PASCAL

Perfection does not exist; to understand it is the triumph of human intelligence; to expect to possess it is the most dangerous kind of madness.

ALFRED de MUSSET

Perfection is attained by slow degrees; it requires the hand of time.

FRANCOIS VOLTAIRE

The essence of being human is that one does not seek perfection.

GEORGE ORWELL

There is a passion for perfection which you will rarely see fully developed; but you may note this fact, that in successful lives it is never wholly lacking.

BLISS CARMAN

It is a great imperfection to complain unceasingly of little things.

SAINT FRANCIS de SALES

Try as hard as we may for perfection, the net result of our labours is an amazing variety of imperfectness. We are surprised at our own versatility in being able to fail in so many different ways.

SAMUEL McCHORD CROTHERS

The roots of true achievement lie in the will to become the best that you can become.

HAROLD TAYLOR

Aim at perfection in everything, though in most things it is unattainable; however, they who aim at it, and persevere will come much nearer to it than those whose laziness and despondency make them give it up as unattainable. LORD CHESTERFIELD

The gem cannot be polished without friction, nor man perfected without trials. CHINESE PROVERB

Human excellence means nothing
Unless it works with the consent of God. EURIPIDES

To reach perfection, we must all pass, one by one, through the death of self-effacement. DAG HAMMARSKJOLD

If thou wilt be perfect, go and sell that thou hast, and give to the poor, and thou shalt have treasure in heaven. *Matthew*

The Fates, like an absent-minded printer, seldom allow a single line to stand perfect and unmarred. GEORGE SANTAYANA

Ideals

If you cannot
Realize your ideal,
Why not try to
Idealize your real?

It is at our mother's knee that we acquire our noblest and truest and highest ideals, but there is seldom any money in them. MARK TWAIN

An idealist is for anything so long as it does not hurt business—his business. ANON

Idealism increases in direct proportion to one's distance from the problem. JOHN GALSWORTHY

An idealist is a person who helps other people to be prosperous.
HENRY FORD

There are only two classes—first class and no class.
DAVID O. SELZNICK

I have never been an idealist—that implies you aren't going to achieve something. ARTHUR SCARGILL

An idealist is one who, on noticing that a rose smells better than a cabbage, concluded that it will also make a better soup.
HENRY LOUIS MENCKEN

I am an idealist. I don't know where I'm going, but I'm on my way.
CARL SANDBURG

Only the mediocre are always at their best. ANON

I have been too lenient. ADOLF HITLER

One of the rarest things that a man ever does is to do the best he can.
JOSH BILLINGS

Don't use that foreign word "Ideals." We have that excellent native word "Lies." HENRIK IBSEN

When they come downstairs from their Ivory Towers, idealists are apt to walk straight into the gutter. LOGAN PEARSALL SMITH

Whatever is—is best. ELLA WHEELER WILCOX

Words without actions are the assassins of idealism.
HERBERT HOOVER

If an ideal is possible it must already be in the thoughts of the people.
ROBERT LOUIS STEVENSON

You must begin with an ideal and end with an ideal.
SIR FREDERICK G. BANTING

The idealist walks on tiptoe, the materialist on his heels.
MALCOLM de CHAZAL

Some people never have anything except ideals.
EDGAR WATSON HOWE

Don't part company with your ideals. They are anchors in a storm.
ARNOLD GLASGOW

No man can be satisfied with his attainment, although he may be satisfied with his circumstances. FRANK SWINNERTON

There is nothing the matter with Americans except their ideals; the real American is all right; it is the ideal American who is all wrong.
GILBERT KEITH CHESTERTON

All men are prepared to accomplish the incredible if their ideals are threatened.
HERMANN HESSE

Idealism is the noble toga that political gentlemen drape over their will to power.
ALDOUS LEONARD HUXLEY

Set up as an ideal the facing of reality as honestly and as cheerfully as possible.
DR. KARL MENNINGER

The idealist is incorrigible; if he is thrown out of his heaven he makes an ideal of his hell.
FRIEDRICH WILHELM NIETZSCHE

I assure you I had rather excel others in the knowledge of what is excellent, than in the extent of my power and dominion.
ALEXANDER the GREAT

A man is no greater than his dream, his ideal, his hope, and his plan. Man dreams the dream—and fulfilling it, it's the dream that makes the man.
ANON

In our ideals we unwittingly reveal our vices.
JEAN ROSTAND

It is not materialism that is the chief curse of the world, as pastors teach, but idealism. Men get into trouble by taking their visions and hallucinations too seriously.
HENRY LOUIS MENCKEN

Conscience

What's a conscience for?
When a bad one
Is seen so much more
Than a good one!

Conscience is the inner voice which warns us that someone may be looking.
HENRY LOUIS MENCKEN

He who has no conscience makes up by lacking it.
STANISLAW J. LEC

Another man within me. THOMAS BROWNE

Conscience: A small, still voice that makes minority reports. FRANKLIN JONES

Man is the only animal that blushes. Or needs to. MARK TWAIN

There is only one way to achieve happiness on this terrestrial ball, and that is to have either a clear conscience, or none at all. OGDEN NASH

It is much easier to repent of sins that we have committed than to repent of those we intend to commit. JOSH BILLINGS

Conscience is thoroughly well-bred and soon leaves off talking to those who do not wish to hear it. SAMUEL BUTLER

Conscience is the voice of your neighbor. FRIEDRICH WILHELM NIETZSCHE

Conscience: something that feels terrible when everything else feels swell. ANON

I have a New England conscience—I like to pay my bills on the second of the month. SINCLAIR LEWIS

If we cannot be powerful and happy and prey on others, we invent conscience and prey on ourselves. ELBERT HUBBARD

My concern is not whether God is on our side; my great concern is to be on God's side. ABRAHAM LINCOLN

Conscience is nothing but other people inside you. LUIGI PIRANDELLO

He had sufficient conscience to bother him, but not sufficient to keep him straight. DAVID LLOYD GEORGE

Conscience cannot prevent sin. It only prevents you from enjoying it. HARRY HERSHFIELD

Most people sell their souls and live with a good conscience on the proceeds. LOGAN PEARSALL SMITH

Resisting temptation is usually just a matter of putting it off until nobody's looking. FRANKLIN JONES

My conscience is more trouble and bother to me than anything else I started with. MARK TWAIN

Conscience is that still small voice that makes you feel even smaller. JAMES A. SANAKER

An evil conscience is often quiet, but never secure. PUBLILIUS SYRUS

Conscience whispers, but interest screams aloud. J. PETIT-SENN

In many walks of life, a conscience is a more expensive encumbrance than a wife or a carriage. THOMAS De QUINCEY

Many people feel "guilty" about things they shouldn't feel guilty about, in order to shut out feelings of guilt about things they should feel guilty about. SYDNEY HARRIS

In the courtroom of our conscience, we call only witnesses for the defense. FRANCOIS MAURIAC

You can let your conscience alone if you're nice to the second housemaid. HENRY JAMES

I cannot and will not cut my conscience to fit this year's fashions. LILLIAN HELLMAN

Conscience and cowardice are really the same things. Conscience is the trade name of the firm. OSCAR WILDE

The bite of conscience teaches men to bite. FRIEDRICH WILHELM NIETZSCHE

One of the greatest sources of suffering is to have an inborn sense of honor. BENJAMIN De CASSERES

The one thing that doesn't abide by a majority rule is a person's conscience. HAROLD LEE

A guilty conscience is a hidden enemy. INDIAN PROVERB

Even when there is no law, there is conscience. PUBLILIUS SYRUS

Conviction is the Conscience of the Mind. MRS. HUMPHREY WARD

Nothing makes it easier to resist temptation than a proper upbringing, a sound set of values, and witnesses. FRANKLIN JONES

Conscience does make cowards of us all. WILLIAM SHAKESPEARE

I have to live with myself, and so
I want to be fit for myself to know;
I want to be able as the days go by,
Always to look myself straight in the eye. EDGAR A. GUEST

Conscience is a cur that will let you get past it but that you cannot keep from barking. ANON

The fact that human conscience remains partially infantile throughout life is the core of human tragedy. ERIK H. ERIKSON

How unhappy is he who cannot forgive himself. PUBLILIUS SYRUS

IX PRINCIPLES

Principles

Principle and stubbornness
Often go together;
Both of them will help you get
Through the stormy weather.

A man is usually more careful of his money than he is of his principles.
EDGAR WATSON HOWE

When a feller says it ain't the money but the principle of the thing, it's the money.
ABE MARTIN

When you say that you agree to a thing in principle, you mean that you have not the slightest intention of carrying it out in practice.
ANON

It is better to be defeated on principle than to win on lies.
ARTHUR R. CALWELL

Not a tenth of us who are in business are doing as well as we could if we merely followed the principles that were known to our grandfathers.
WILLIAM FEATHER

He'll doublecross that bridge when he comes to it.
OSCAR LEVANT

Moral principle is a looser bond than pecuniary interest.
ABRAHAM LINCOLN

Principles always become a matter of vehement discussion when practice is at an ebb. GEORGE GISSING

In any assembly the simplest way to stop the transacting of business and split the ranks is to appeal to a principle. JACQUES BARZUN

We should not wrap ourselves in a banner of so-called principle when we are really concerned only with economic advantage.
J. L. McCAFFREY

I don't believe in principles but I do in interest.
JAMES RUSSELL LOWELL

Prosperity is the best protector of principle. MARK TWAIN

I have been a selfish being all my life, in practice, though not in principle. JANE AUSTEN

The procedures of modern management have become enormously complex but the principles remain the same. CLARENCE FRANCIS

It is often easier to fight for principles than to live up to them.
ADLAI STEVENSON

An Englishman does everything on principle: he fights you on patriotic principles; he robs you on business principles; he enslaves you on imperial principles. GEORGE BERNARD SHAW

I have a simple principle for the conduct of life—never to resist an adequate temptation. MAX LERNER

In life as in a football game, the principle to follow is: Hit the line hard!
THEODORE ROOSEVELT

Amid the pressure of great events, a general principle gives no help.
GEORG FRIEDRICH WILHELM NEGEL

Principles have no real force except when one is well fed.
MARK TWAIN

Expedients are for the hour, but principles are for the ages.
HENRY WARD BEECHER

The secret of prosperity in common life is to be commonplace on principle. WALTER BAGEHOT

Ethics

When you're considering any sort of temptation,
You should think hard about your reputation.
Then make up your mind with no hesitation
To turn it down firmly without reservation.
If another good chance is your expectation,
You can try it again at the next presentation.

The quality of moral behaviour varies in inverse ratio to the number of human beings involved. ALDOUS LEONARD HUXLEY

There is no admission charge to the straight and narrow path. ANON

It is not best that we use our morals week days; it gets them out of repair for Sundays. MARK TWAIN

The truth is, hardly any of us have ethical energy enough for more than one really inflexible point of honor. GEORGE BERNARD SHAW

Good resolutions are simply checks that men draw on a bank where they have no account. OSCAR WILDE

Thou canst not serve both cod and salmon. ADA LEVERSON

Without doubt half the ethical rules they din into our ears are designed to keep us at work. LLEWELLYN POWYS

Men of business must not break their word twice. THOMAS FULLER

Always do right. This will surprise some people and astonish the rest. MARK TWAIN

It makes a great difference whether a person is unwilling to sin, or does not know how. LUCIUS ANNAEUS SENECA

Gamesmanship, or The Art of Winning Games Without Actually Cheating. STEPHEN POTTER

The best way to keep your word is not to give it. NAPOLEON BONAPARTE

Most people are good only so long as they believe others to be so.
FRIEDRICH HEBBEL

The first step in the evolution of ethics is a sense of solidarity with other human beings. ALBERT SCHWEITZER

The only way to get rid of a temptation is to yield to it. Resist it, and your soul grows sick with longing for the things it has forbidden to itself.
OSCAR WILDE

Faith makes many of the mountains which it has to remove.
DEAN WILLIAM RALPH INGE

The strength of a man's virtue should not be measured by his special exertions, but by his habitual acts. BLAISE PASCAL

Be good and you will be lonesome. MARK TWAIN

Would that the simple maxim, that honesty is the best policy, might be laid to heart; that a sense of the true aim of life might elevate the tone of politics and trade till public and private honor become identical.
MARGARET FULLER

Never esteem anything as of advantage to thee that shall make thee break thy word or lose thy self-respect. MARCUS AURELIUS

If your morals make you dreary, depend on it they are wrong.
ROBERT LOUIS STEVENSON

Where wealth and freedom reign, contentment fails,
And honour sinks where commerce long prevails.
OLIVER GOLDSMITH

Industry stands for the good life, for the social and economic betterment of all, for the proposition that to produce more with the same amount of human effort is a sound social and economic objective. Business and industry's position in this respect rests squarely upon the ethical and moral concept of dignity of the individual employee. ANON

Honesty

Trust all men with vigilance,
If that's the way you feel;
Perhaps they never had the chance
To get away with it and steal.

Honesty is the best policy when there's money in it. MARK TWAIN

There's one way to find out if a man is honest—ask him. If he says "yes" you know he is crooked. GROUCHO MARX

It is difficult but not impossible to conduct strictly honest business. What is true is that honesty is incompatible with the amassing of a large fortune. MOHANDAS K. GANDHI

It is not the crook in modern business that we fear, but the honest man who doesn't know what he is doing. OWEN D. YOUNG

Nothing is quite honest that is not commercial, but not everything commercial is honest. ROBERT FROST

Honesty—after the first million! QUINTUS FLACCUS HORACE

If you can't give me your word of honor, will you give me your promise? SAMUEL GOLDWYN

Perhaps honesty may not be the best policy . . . but it's the safest. EDWARD H. HARRIMAN

The surest way to remain poor is to be an honest man. NAPOLEON BONAPARTE

Let none of us delude himself by supposing that honesty is always the best policy. It is not. DEAN WILLIAM RALPH INGE

Honesty is a good thing but it is not profitable to its possessor unless it is kept under control. DONALD ROBERT PERRY MARWUIS

Honesty is the rarest wealth anyone can possess, and yet all the honesty in the world ain't lawful tender for a loaf of bread. JOSH BILLINGS

If honesty did not exist, we ought to invent it as the best means of getting rich.
HONORE GABRIEL MIRABEAU

Make yourself an honest man and then you may be sure there is one rascal less in the world.
THOMAS CARLYLE

We ought never to do wrong when people are looking. MARK TWAIN

He is only honest who is not discovered. SUSANNA CENTILIVRE

It takes a wise man to handle a lie. A fool had better remain honest.
NORMAN DOUGLAS

Even the best-intentioned of great men need a few scoundrels around them, there are some things you cannot ask an honest man to do.
JEAN de la BRUYÈRE

Though I am not naturally honest, I am so sometimes by chance.
WILLIAM SHAKESPEARE

Confidence in others' honesty is no light testimony of one's own integrity.
MICHEL de MONTAIGNE

The nearest way to honour is to have none at all. SAMUEL BUTLER

Honesty's praised, then left to freeze. DECIMUS JUNIUS JUVENAL

An honest man's word is as good as his bond.
MIGUEL de CERVANTES

God defend me from being an honest man according to the description which every day I see made by each man to his own glorification.
MICHAEL de MONTAIGNE

People who honestly mean to be true, really contradict themselves much more rarely than those who try to be "consistent."
OLIVER WENDELL HOLMES

"Honesty" without compassion and understanding, is not honesty, but subtle hostility.
DR. ROSE N. FRANZBLAU

Dishonesty

Dishonesty often
Has one little quirk;
It may be a way of
Avoiding hard work.

Money dishonestly acquired is never worth its cost, while a good conscience never costs as much as it is worth. J. P. SENN

If you rob Peter to pay Paul you can always depend on the support of Paul. LAURENCE J. PETER

Opportunity makes the thief. ENGLISH PROVERB

I shall never forget my mother's horror and my father's cry of joy when, for the first time in my life, I said angrily to my father, "That's not the hand I dealt you, Dad." J. B. MORTON

Steal from one person and it's plagiarism; steal from four people and it's scholarship. WILSON MIZNER

The rain it raineth on the just
  And also on the unjust fella;
But chiefly on the just, because
  The unjust steals the just's umbrella. BARON CHARLES BOWEN

Feel for others, in your pocket. AMERICAN PROVERB

He that steals an egg will steal an ox. EDMUND FULLER

The world will be a better place when the Found ads in the newspapers begin to out number the Lost ads. LISA KIRK

At first we thought the world was flat. Next we decided it was round. Today we know it is crooked. LEOPOLD FECHTNER

If a thing's worth having, it's worth cheating for. W. C. FIELDS

Thieves hunt in couples but a liar alone. AMERICAN PROVERB

The Eleventh Commandment: Thou shalt not be found out.
GEORGE WHYTE MELVILLE

It is a trick among the dishonest to offer sacrifices that are not needed, or not possible, to avoid making those that are required.
IVAN GONCHAROV

Nobody really loves to be cheated, but it does seem as though everyone is anxious to see how near he could come to it. JOSH BILLINGS

There's a lot of things blamed on me that never happened. But then, there's a lot of things that I did and never got caught at.
JOHNNY CASH

Whatever is not nailed down is mine
Whatever I can pry loose is not nailed down.
COLLIS P. HUNTINGTON

I have known a vast quantity of nonsense talked about bad men not looking you in the face. Don't trust that conventional idea. Dishonesty will stare honesty out of countenance, any day in the week, if there is anything to be got by it. CHARLES DICKENS

Many a man is saved from being a thief by finding everything locked up.
EDGAR WATSON HOWE

I never cheated an honest man, only rascals. They wanted something for nothing. I gave them nothing for something.
JOSEPH "YELLOW KID" WEIL

It is not easy to steal where the landlord is a thief. IRISH PROVERB

You are not to do evil that good may come of it. LEGAL MAXIM

What's left over from the thief is spent on the fortune-teller.
YIDDISH PROVERB

Sooner of later false thinking brings wrong conduct. JULIAN HUXLEY

Hope of ill gain is the beginning of loss. DEMOCRITUS

Mundus vult decipi decipiatur ergo. The world wants to be cheated, so cheat. XAVIERA HOLLANDER

Highways and streets have not all the thieves; shops have ten for one.
ENGLISH PROVERB

The Devil makes his Christmas pie of lawyers' tongues and clerks' fingers.
ANON

He that mischief hatcheth, mischief catcheth. WILLIAM CAMDEN

Prefer loss to the wealth of dishonest gain; the former vexes you for a time, the later will bring you lasting remorse. CHILO

If you know that a thing is unrighteous, then use all dispatch in putting an end to it—why wait till next year? MENCIUS

Fraud

The cash register
Will resist a
Twister.

There are no new forms of financial fraud; in the last several hundred years, there have only been small variations on a few classic designs.
JOHN KENNETH GALBRAITH

Commerce is the school of cheating. MARQUIS de VAUVENARGUES

Some are born good,
Some make good, and some
Are caught with the goose. LAURENCE J. PETER

Make money, money by fair means if you can, if not, by any means money. QUINTUS FLACCUS HORACE

When the ruins of Pompeii were uncovered, dice were found. It is a sad commentary on the unvarying conditions of human nature that some of those dice were loaded. LORD KILMUIR

I liked the store detective who said he's seen a lot of people who were so confused that they'd stolen things, but never one so confused that they'd paid twice. BARONESS PHILLIPS

Cheat neat. RICHARD PETTY

The illegal we do immediately. The unconstitutional takes a bit longer. HENRY KISSINGER

For de little stealin' day gits you in jail soon or late. For de big stealin' day makes you emperor and puts you in de Hall o' Fame when you croaks. EUGENE O'NEIL

Executive to employee: "I can't approve your expense account, Jones, but we'd like to buy the fiction rights to it." NORMAN WEED

A false balance is abomination to the Lord but a just weight is his delight. PROVERBS

Hand, n: A singular instrument worn at the end of a human arm, and commonly thrust into somebody's pocket. AMBROSE BIERCE

The usual trade and commerce is cheating all round by consent. THOMAS FULLER

It is more dangerous to be a great prophet or poet than to promote twenty companies for swindling simple folk out of their savings. GEORGE BERNARD SHAW

A retired industrial tycoon, talking to his listless grandson, said, "Why don't you go out and look for a job? Why, when I was your age, I was working for $3 a week. At the end of five years, I owned the store."

"You can't do that now," was the lackadaisical reply. "They have cash registers." OLGA J. FERT

Cheating: It is almost always worthwhile to be cheated; people's little frauds have an interest which more than repays what they cost us. LOGAN PEARSALL SMITH

You have to prevent yourself from being conned so you don't con other people. BILLY IDOL

It is impossible to cheat life; there are no answers to the problems of life in the back of the book. SOREN KIERKEGAARD

Don't steal: thou'll never thus compete successfully in business. Cheat.
AMBROSE BIERCE

Those people who hold the strongest convictions are often behind bars.
ANON

Rodeoing is about the only sport you can't fix. You'd have to talk to the bulls and horses, and they wouldn't understand you.
BILL LINDERMAN

He that will cheat at play
Will cheat you any way.
ANON

There are some frauds so well conducted that it would be stupidity not to be deceived by them.
CHARLES CALEB COLTON

He who will not apply himself to business, evidently discovers that he means to get his bread by cheating, stealing, or begging, or else is wholly void of reason.
ISCHOMACHUS

Lines of least resistance make crooked rivers and crooked men.
WILLIAM H. DANFORTH

The first and worst of all frauds is to cheat oneself.
GAMALIEL BAILEY

'Tis my opinion every man cheats in his way, and he is only honest who is not discovered.
SUSANNAH CENTILIVRE

It is not a sin to sell dear, but it is to make ill measure.
EDMUND FULLER

Fraud generally lights a candle for justice to get a look at it; and a rogue's pen indites the warrant for his own arrest.
ANON

The more gross the fraud the more glibly will it go down, and the more greedily be swallowed, since folly will always find faith where impostors will find impudence.
CHARLES CALEB COLTON

Whoever has even once become notorious by base fraud, even if he speaks the truth, gains no belief.
PHAEDRUS

Corruption

Those who think
Money
Will do anything
Are the same
Who will
Do anything for
Money.

I am like any other man. All I do is supply a demand. AL CAPONE

Men are more often bribed by their loyalties and ambitions than by money. ROBERT H. JACKSON

I have observed there is a difference between the Irish Mafia and the Texas Mafia. You may still receive the knife but you get prayed over in the process. ERIC SEVAREID

Crime is a logical extension of the sort of behaviour that is often considered perfectly respectable in legitimate business. ROBERT RICE

Democracy substitutes election by the incompetent many for appointment by the corrupt few. GEORGE BERNARD SHAW

I own Chicago. I own Miami. I own Las Vegas. SAM GIANCANA

Business men must learn they cannot be in bed with elements of organized crime and then when trouble comes just say they are sorry. JUDGE ARNOLD BAUMAN

Money is good for bribing your way through the inconveniences of life. GOTTFRIED REINHARDT

There is no racketeering like there was years ago. It is all make believe. BARNEY BAKER

Public money is like holy water; everyone helps himself to it. ITALIAN PROVERB

Nobody takes a bribe. Of course, at Christmas, if you happen to hold out your hat and somebody happens to put a little something in it, well, that's different. POLICE COMMISSIONER WILLIAM P. O'BRIEN

Few men have virtue to withstand the highest bidder.
GEORGE WASHINGTON

The first sign of corruption in a society that is still alive is that the end justifies the means. GEORGE BERNANOS

God looks at the clean hands, not the full ones. PUBLILIUS SYRUS

Bribes will enter without knocking. BRITISH PROVERB

All those men have their price. SIR ROBERT WALPOLE

A friend that you buy with presents will be bought from you.
THOMAS FULLER

If one offers money to a government to influence it, that is corruption. But if someone receives money for services rendered afterward, that is a commission. ADRIAN KHASHOGGI

Corruption: Bad officials are ones elected by good citizens who do not vote. GEORGE JEAN NATHAN

A shady business never yields a sunny life. B. C. FORBES

I needed the goodwill of the legislature of four states. I "formed" the legislative bodies with my own money. I found that it was cheaper that way. JAY GOULD

Still, as of old, men by themselves are priced
For thirty pieces Judas sold himself, not Christ.
HESTER H. CHOLMONDELEY

One now and then meets with people on whose face, in whose manner, in whose words, one may read a bill giving notice that they are to be let or sold. They also profess to be furnished, but everybody knows what the furniture of a ready-furnished house usually is. JULIUS HARE

The typical American believes that no necessity of the soul is free, and that there are precious few, if any, which cannot be bought.
JOSEPH WOOD KRUTCH

It is probably safe to say that over a long period of time political morality has been as high as business morality. HENRY STEELE COMMAGER

The door will not open to words, and it is only a well-fidded palm that should do the knocking. ALBIUS TIBULLUS

The accomplice to the crime of corruption is frequently our own indifference. BESS MYERSON

He that bringeth a present findeth the door open. THOMAS FULLER

He who receives a benefit should never forget it: he who bestows should never remember it. PIERRE CHARRON

Corruption is like a ball of snow whence once set a-rolling it must increase. CHARLES CALEB COLTON

The American way is to seduce a man by bribery and make a prostitute of him. Or else to ignore him, starve him into submission and make a hack out of him. HENRY MILLER

Corruption, the most infallible sympton of constitutional liberty.
EDWARD GIBBON

They that buy an office must sell something. THOMAS FULLER

A greased mouth cannot say no. ITALIAN PROVERB

Honesty stands at the gate and knocks, and bribery enters in. ANON

It is unquestionably possible for an incorruptable man to succeed in business. But his scruples are an embarrassment. He must make up in ability for what he lacks in moral obliquity. JOHN JAY CHAPMAN

Corruption wins not more than honesty. WILLIAM SHAKESPEARE

Hope of ill gain is the beginning of loss. DEMOCRITUS

They say the gods themselves are moved by gifts, and gold does more with men than words. EURIPIDES

Using vile means to attain worthy ends makes the ends themselves vile.
ANTON CHEKHOV

Gain not base gains, base gains are the same as losses. HESIOD

He that is extravagant will soon become poor, and poverty will enforce dependence, and invite corruption. SAMUEL JOHNSON

An official never flogs a bearer of gifts. CHINESE PROVERB

There is no odor so bad as that which arises from goodness tainted. HENRY DAVID THOREAU

Reputation

The name's the game,
So get the knack
To sift your fame
Of what you lack.

A man is always stronger while he is making a reputation than he is after it is made. JOSH BILLINGS

Reputation is a bubble which a man bursts when he tries to blow it for himself. EMMA CARLETON

Character is made by what you stand for; reputation by what you fall for. ROBERT QUILLEN

A man is known by the company he organizes. AMBROSE BIERCE

A company is judged by the president it keeps. JAMES HULBERT

The art of life is to be so well known at a good restaurant that you can pay with a check. E. V. LUCAS

Nothing inspires confidence in a business man sooner than punctuality, nor is there any habit which sooner saps his reputation than that of always being behind time. WILLIAM MATTHEWS

The only time you realize you have a reputation is when you're not living up to it. JOSE ITURBI

An Englishman asked a Jew why his race were said to be so mercenary and was told that, maybe, it was for the same reason that his countrymen were said to be gentlemen.
ANON

Every man has a lurking wish to appear considerable in his native place.
SAMUEL JOHNSON

People are only heroes when they cannot do anything else.
PAUL CLAUDEL

Private faces in public places
Are wiser and nicer
Than public faces in private places.
WYSTAN HUGH AUDEN

Many a man's reputation would not know his character if they met on the street.
ELBERT HUBBARD

If I take care of my character, my reputation will take care of itself.
D. L. MOODY

It is hardly respectable to be good nowadays.
EDITH SITWELL

If I am a great man, then a good many of the great men of history are frauds.
BONAR LAW

Character is what you have;
reputation is what you get caught at.
ANON

The worst thing that can happen to a man is to lose his money, the next worst is his health, the next worst his reputation.
SAMUEL BUTLER

Fame is proof that the people are gullible.
RALPH WALDO EMERSON

Respectability: the offspring of a liaison between bald head and bank account.
AMBROSE BIERCE

I never did anything to deserve that reputation unless it was to supply good beer to people who wanted it.
DUTCH SCHULTZ

Reputation is commonly measured by the acre.
THOMAS FULLER

What a heavy burden is a name that has become too famous.
FRANCOIS VOLTAIRE

The more things a man is ashamed of, the more respectable he is.
GEORGE BERNARD SHAW

Respectable means rich, and decent means poor. I should die if I heard my family called decent. THOMAS LOVE PEACOCK

Don't speak either too well or too bad of yourself. If well, men will not believe you; if bad, they will believe a great deal more than you say.
ANON

Fame isn't a thing. It's a feeling. Like what you get after a pill.
JOYCE CAREY

A single lie destroys a whole reputation for integrity.
BALTASAR GRACIAN

A name is a kind of face whereby one is known. THOMAS FULLER

To enjoy a good reputation, give publicly, and steal privately.
JOSH BILLINGS

Reputation is like credit—it enables one to venture on enterprises which else it were rash to undertake. JOHN LANCASTER SPALDING

When people have heard of you, favorably or not, they change.
JOHN STEINBECK

It is generally much more shameful to lose a good reputation than never to have acquired it. PLINY the YOUNGER

It is harder to live up to a reputation than it is to die for a principle.
ANON

What I must do is all that concerns me, not what the people think.
RALPH WALDO EMERSON

Either a good or a bad reputation outruns and gets before people wherever they go. EARL OF CHESTERFIELD

Nothing got without pains but an ill name and long nails.
SCOTTISH PROVERB

Character is like a tree, and reputation like its shadow. The shadow is what we think of it; the tree is the real thing. ANON

It is a sign that your reputation is small and sinking, if your own tongue must praise you. MATTHEW HALE

Public opinion, a vulgar, impertinent, anonymous tyrant who deliberately makes life unpleasant for anyone who is not content to be the average man. DEAN WILLIAM RALPH INGE

Reputation is an idle and most false imposition, oft got without merit, and lost without deserving. WILLIAM SHAKESPEARE

Have regard for your name, since it will remain for you longer than a great store of fold. *Ecclesiasticus*

Open your mouth and purse cautiously, and your stock of wealth and reputation shall, at least in repute, be great.
JOHANN GEORG von ZIMMERMANN

Are you not ashamed of heaping up the greatest amount of money and honor and reputation, and caring so little about wisdom and truth and the greatest improvement of the soul, which you never regard or heed at all?
SOCRATES

Simplicity

Even a pimple
Is not simple.

Progress is man's ability to complicate simplicity.
THOR HEYERDAHL

Seek simplicity and distrust it. ALFRED NORTH WHITEHEAD

Keep it simple, stupid. AXIOM OF ISRAELI AIR FORCE

The greatest results in life are usually attained by simple means and the exercise of ordinary qualities. These may for the most part be summed up in these two—common sense and perseverance. OWEN FEITHAM

Simplicity is an exact medium between too little and too much.
JOSHUA REYNOLDS

Everything should be made as simple as possible, but not one bit simpler.
ALBERT EINSTEIN

If you simplify one item, you exaggerate the rest.
ANDRE GIDE

There is more simplicity in the man who eats caviar on impulse than in the man who eats grapenuts on principle.
GILBERT KEITH CHESTERTON

The greatest truths are the simplest: and so are the greatest men.
JULIUS CHARLES HARE and AUGUSTUS WILLIAM HARE

If it ain't broke, don't fix it.
BERT LANCE

The ability to simplify means to eliminate the unnecessary so that the necessary may speak.
HANS HOFMANN

Our life is frittered away by detail. . . . Simplify, simplify.
HENRY DAVID THOREAU

It is the essence of genius to make use of the simplest ideas.
CHARLES PEGUY

Simplicity, of all things, is the hardest to be copied.
SIR RICHARD STEELE

A taste for simplicity cannot endure for long.
EUGENE DELACROIX

You know I say just what I think, and nothing more or less. I cannot say one thing and mean another.
HENRY WADSWORTH LONGFELLOW

To be simple is the best thing in the world: to be modest is the next best thing. I am not so sure about being quiet.
GILBERT KEITH CHESTERTON

Men who have been in battle know from first-hand experience that when the chips are down, a man fights to help the man next to him, just as a company fights to keep pace with its flanks. Things have to be that simple.
S. L. A. MARSHALL

You should avoid making yourself too clear even in your explanations.
BALTASAR GRACIAN

As soon as you are complicated, your are ineffectual.
KONRAD ADENAUER

The best ways are the most straightforward ways. When you're sitting around scamming these things out, all kinds of James Bondian ideas come forth, but when it gets down to the reality of it, the simplest and most straightforward way is usually the best, and the way that attracts the least attention. THOMAS KING FORCADE

Out of intense complexities intense simplicities emerge.
SIR WINSTON CHURCHILL

Nothing is more simple than greatness: indeed, to be simple is to be great. RALPH WALDO EMERSON

Simplicity, simplicity, simplicity! I say, let your affairs be as two or three, and not a hundred or a thousand: instead of a million, count half a dozen, and keep your accounts on your thumbnail.
HENRY DAVID THOREAU

Truth

Every time the truth is stretched
And you try to overdo it,
It all appears so farfetched
That everyone sees through it.

When money speaks the truth is silent. RUSSIAN PROVERB

There are 869 different forms of lying but only one of them has been squarely forbidden: thou shalt not bear false witness against thy neighbour. MARK TWAIN

It makes all the difference in the world whether we put truth in the first place, or in the second place. JOHN MORLEY

I'm not smart enough to lie. RONALD REAGAN

One of the advantages of telling the truth is that you need not remember what you said. LORD BIRKETT

The truth is where the truth is, and it's sometimes in the candy store. BOB DYLAN

Men occasionally stumble over the truth, but most of them pick themselves up and hurry off as if nothing had happened. WINSTON CHURCHILL

How is it that George Washington slept so many places and yet never told a lie? LAURENCE J. PETER

It may almost be held that the hope of commercial gain has done nearly as much for the cause of truth, as even the love of truth itself. CHRISTIAN NESTELL BOVEE

There are a terrible lot of lies going about the world, and the worst of it is that half of them are true. ANON

He not only doesn't give a damn about the people: he doesn't know how to tell the truth. I don't think the son of a bitch knows the difference between telling the truth and lying. HARRY S. TRUMAN

Lying is not taxed. SPANISH PROVERB

An American who can make money, invoke God, and be no better than his neighbor, has nothing to fear but truth itself. MARYA MANNES

The pure and simple truth is rarely pure and never simple. OSCAR WILDE

Truth is something you stumble into when you think you're going someplace else. JERRY GARCIA

What is intended as a little white lie often ends up as a double feature in Technicolor. MADENA R. WALLINGFORD

If everything they say I've done was true, I'd be in a penitentiary long ago. JERRY LEE LEWIS

He who tells the truth should have one foot in the stirrup.
ARAB PROVERB

"I want an explanation and I want the truth."
"Make up your mind. You can't have both." JACOB M. BRAUDE

In this world, truth can wait; she's used to it. DOUGLAS JERROLD

Truth: something somehow discreditable to someone.
HENRY LOUIS MENCKEN

It must be Sunday
Everybody's telling the truth. . . . PHOEBE SNOW

Truth. Sir, is a cow which will yield such sceptics, no more milk, and so they are gone to milk the bull. SAMUEL JOHNSON

Often, the surest way to convey misinformation is to tell the strict truth.
MARK TWAIN

Like all valuable commodities, truth is often counterfeited.
JAMES CARDINAL GIBBONS

A lie can be half-way round the world before the truth has got its boots on. JAMES CALLAGHAN

Pretty much all the honest truthtelling there is in the world is done by children. ANON

The truth is more important than the facts. FRANK LLOYD WRIGHT

Truth exists. Only lies are invented. GEORGE BRAQUE

The truth would become more popular if it were not always stating ugly facts. HENRY S. HASKINS

One can live in this world on soothsaying but not on truthsaying.
GEORG CHRISTOPH LICHTENBERG

You will find that the truth is often unpopular and the contest between agreeable fancy and disagreeable fact is unequal for, in the vernacular, we Americans are suckers for good news. ADLAI STEVENSON

Truth often suffers more by the heat of its defenders than from the arguments of its opposers. WILLIAM PENN

Chase after truth like hell and you'll free yourself, even though you never touch its coat-tails. CLARENCE DARROW

Show me a liar, and I will show thee a thief. GEORGE HERBERT

When I tell any truth, it is not for the sake of convincing those who do not know it, but for the sake of defending those that do.
WILLIAM BLAKE

Every truth passes through three stages before it is recognized. In the first it is ridiculed, in the second it is opposed, in the third it is regarded as self-evident. ARTHUR SCHOPENHAUER

Why should I tell the truth if it makes us look like schmucks in comparison to a liar. I lie only to correct the perspective. What are you supposed to do? Go to eight thousand people in entertainment and say, "Be honest." There are more important causes in the world. I didn't write the rules. I just live by them. IRVING AZOFF

Truth emerges more readily from error than from confusion.
FRANCIS BACON

Everyone wishes to have the truth on his side, but not everyone wishes to be on the side of truth. RICHARD WHATELY

It is doubly pleasing to deceive the deceiver. JEAN de la FONTAINE

What has not been examined impartially has not been well examined. Skepticism is therefore the first step toward truth. DENIS DIDEROT

There are some persons who would not for their lives tell a direct and wilful lie, but who so exaggerate that it seems as if for their lives they could not tell the exact truth. EUSEBIUS PAGET

It is one of the maladies of our age to profess a frenzied allegiance to truth in unimportant matters, to refuse consistently to face her where graver issues are at stake. NORMAN DOUGLAS

Look to the Classics, History, to the Arts, for there is the truth.
Look away from the system, the processes, the techniques.
CHARLES GUGGENHEIM

The feller that calls you "brother" generally wants something that don't belong to him. FRANK McKINNEY HUBBARD

The biggest liar in the world is They Say. DOUGLAS MALLOCK

It is easier to be dishonest for two than for one. JOHN FOWLES

Remember: one lie does not cost you one truth but the truth.
FRIEDRICH HEBBEL

I do not mind lying, but I hate inaccuracy. SAMUEL BUTLER

It is not difficult to deceive a deceiver. JEAN de la FONTAINE

Men hate those to whom they have to lie. VICTOR HUGO

George Washington couldn't tell a lie. I can: but I won't.
MARK TWAIN

We are never so easily deceived as when we imaging we are deceiving others. FRANCOIS DUC de la ROCHEFOUCAULD

Lie lustily, some filth will stick. THOMAS HALL

A man had rather have a hundred lies told about him, than one truth which he does not wish should be told. SAMUEL JOHNSON

I could more easily believe two Yankee professors would lie than stones would fall from heaven. THOMAS JEFFERSON

Everything that deceives may be said to enchant. PLATO

In real life truth is revealed by parables and falsehood supported by facts. GEORGE BERNARD SHAW

How does a person get to be a capable liar?
That is something that I respectfully inquiar,
Because I don't believe a person will ever set the world on fire
Unless they are a capable lire. OGDEN NASH

One comes, finally, to believe whatever one repeats to one's self, whether the statement is true or false. NAPOLEON HILL

No man was ever so much deceived by another as by himself.
LORD GREVILLE

Deceive not thy physician, confessor, nor lawyer.
GEORGE HERBERT

We are never deceived; we deceive ourselves.
JOHANN WOLFGANG von GOETHE

I cannot tell what part of me deceives the other. GEORG BUCHNER

Nothing is more criminal, mean, or ridiculous, than lying. It is the production either of malice, cowardice or vanity: but it generally misses of its aim in everyone of these views: for lies are always detected sooner or later. LORD CHESTERFIELD

If I accustom a servant to tell a lie for me, have I not reason to apprehend that he will tell many lies for himself? SAMUEL JOHNSON

If you want your deceit to succeed, pretend love and loyalty; keep a dagger under your cloak, ready to administer the coup de grace, at the first opportunity, to the man who trusts you!
GIAMBATTISTA CINTHIO GIRALDI

Sincerity is an opening of the heart; we find it in very few persons, and that which we see ordinarily is only a cunning deceit to attract the confidence of others. FRANCOIS DUC de la ROCHEFOUCAULD

X DANGERS

Error

Completely wrong
In the short term
Is better than
Partially wrong
In the long term.

The 1976 Olympics could no more lose money than I could have a baby.
MAYOR OF MONTREAL

The man who has never done any harm will never do any good.
GEORGE BERNARD SHAW

Things could be worse. Suppose your errors were counted and published every day, like those of a baseball player. ANON

If all else fails, immortality can always be assured by spectacular error.
JOHN KENNETH GALBRAITH

Men in high places in industry, government, radio, press, etc., can often spread enough error in a day to keep the forces of enlightenment busy for a year. GLENN D. HOOVER

There is no right way to the wrong thing. OREN ARNOLD

There is nothing more certain than that age and youth are right, except perhaps that both are wrong. ROBERT LOUIS STEVENSON

May I join you in the doghouse, Rover?
I wish to retire till the party's over. OGDEN NASH

The Coca-Cola Co. discovered that it had inadvertently bought Columbia Pictures Inc. Company executives had thought they were buying Colombia, the Central America country. Coca-Cola is asking the movie company for its deposit back. *Off the Wall Street Journal*

How often have I been able to trace bankrupticies and insolvencies to some lawsuit about ten or fifteen pounds, the costs of which have mounted up to large sums. HENRY PETER BROUGHAM

For the sin ye do by two and two ye must pay for one by one. RUDYARD KIPLING

Freedom is the right to be wrong, not the right to do wrong. JOHN DIEFENBAKER

The errors of young men are the ruin of business, but the errors of aged men amount to this, that more might have been done, or sooner. FRANCIS BACON

Error itself may be happy chance. ALFRED NORTH WHITEHEAD

Error will slip through a crack, while truth will stick in a dorrway. HENRY WHEELER SHAW

To err is human, but when the eraser wears out ahead of the pencil, you're overdoing it. J. JENKINS

Delay is preferable to error. THOMAS JEFFERSON

Error is always in haste. THOMAS FULLER

It is the culprit who must seek the glance of the judge, and not the judge that must look at the culprit. JULIA KAVANAGH

The errors of great men are venerable because they are more fruitful than the truths of little men. FRIEDRICH WILHELM NIETZSCHE

The world always makes the assumption that the exposure of an error is identical with the discovery of the truth—that error and truth are simply opposite. They are nothing of the sort. What the world turns to, when it has been cured of one error, is usually simply another error, and maybe one worse than the first one. HENRY LOUIS MENCKEN

Give me a good fruitful error any time, full of seeds, bursting with its own corrections. You can keep your sterile truth for yourself.
VILFREDO PARETO

No sensible person ever makes an apology.
RALPH WALDO EMERSON

In a narrow sphere great men are blunderers.
NAPOLEON BONAPARTE

He who is wrong fights against himself. EGYPTIAN PROVERB

What I want is men who will support me when I am in the wrong.
LORD MELBOURNE

To err is human, to forgive divine. ALEXANDER POPE

The offender never pardons GEORGE HERBERT

Nothing hurts a new truth more than an old error.
JOHANN WOLFGANG von GOETHE

An error is simply a failure to adjust immediately from a preconception to an actuality. JOHN CAGE

It is one thing to show a man that he is in error, and another to put him in possession of the truth. JOHN LOCKE

There is nothing that you and I make so many blunders about, and the world so few, as the actual amount of our importance. JOSH BILLINGS

Freedom is not worth having if it does not connote freedom to err.
MAHATMA GANDHI

One cannot too soon forget his errors and misdemeanors; for to dwell upon them is to add to the offense. HENRY DAVID THOREAU

Irrationally held truths may be more harmful than reasoned errors.
THOMAS H. HUXLEY

My principal method for defeating error and heresy is, by establishing the truth. One purposes to fill a bushel with tares, but if I can fill it first with wheat, I may defy his attempts. JOHN NEWTON

The weak have one weapon: the errors of those who think they are strong.
GEORGES BIDAULT

There is no such source of error as the pursuit of absolute truth.
SAMUEL BUTLER

When the most insignificant person tells us we are in error, we should listen, and examine ourselves, and see if it is so. To believe it possible we may be in error, is the first step toward getting out of it.
JOHANN K. LAVATER

Love truth and pardon error. FRANCOIS VOLTAIRE

Look upon the errors of others in sorrow, not in anger.
HENRY WADSWORTH LONGFELLOW

Caution

When you take care
Not to spill a drop,
Better beware
Not to drop the lot.

Much coin, much care. LATIN PROVERB

Action makes more fortunes than caution.
MARQUIS de VAUVENARGUES

Don't take the bull by the horns, take him by the tail; then you can let him go when you want to. JOSH BILLINGS

The cautious seldom err. CONFUCIUS

He neither drank, smoked, nor rode a bicycle. Living frugally, saving his money, he died early, surrounded by greedy relatives. It was a great lesson to me. JOHN BARRYMORE

The only way to be absolutely safe is never to try anything for the first time. DR. MAGNUS PYKE

It is doubtful if anyone ever made a success of anything who waited until all conditions were "just right" before starting. JACOB M. BRAUDE

There is not much satisfaction in any gain that is achieved by always playing it safe. ANON

Don't be afraid to take a big step if one is indicated; you can't cross a chasm in two small jumps. DAVID LLOYD GEORGE

You might as well fall flat on your face as lean over too far backwards.
JAMES THURBER

The coward regards himself as cautious; the miser, as thrifty.
PUBLILIUS SYRUS

The more wary you are of danger, the more likely you are to meet it.
JEAN de la FONTAINE

Baby, let me say this. I got one eye, and that one eye sees a lot of things that my brain tells me I shouldn't talk about. Because my brain says that, if I do, my one eye might not be seeing anything after a while.
SAMMY DAVIS, JR.

When one finds oneself in the middle of a minefield, it is seldom wise to get up and run. MICHAEL HOWARD

It is only theory that makes men completely incautious.
BERNARD RUSSELL

Monotony is the awful reward of the careful. A. G. BUCKHAM

It is when all play safe that we create a world of utmost insecurity.
DAG HAMMARSKJOLD

People wish to learn to swim and at the same time to keep one foot on the ground. MARCEL PROUST

He who hesitates is sometimes saved. JAMES THURBER

It is a good thing to learn caution by the misfortune of others.
PUBLILIUS SYRUS

The chief danger in life is that you may take too many precautions.
ALFRED ADLER

It is human nature to stand in the middle of a thing.
MARIANNE MOORE

Some fellows get credit for being conservative when they are only stupid.
FRANK McKINNEY HUBBARD

The best armor is to keep out of gunshot. FRANCIS BACON

Cats love fish but do not want to get their feet wet. LATIN PROVERB

He that will not sail till all dangers are over must never put to sea.
THOMAS FULLER

Never measure the height of a mountain until you have reached the top. Then you will see how low it is. DAG HAMMARSKJOLD

If you shut your door to all errors, truth will be shut out.
RABINDRANATH TAGORE

He that observeth the wind shall not sow, and he that regards the clouds shall not reap. *Ecclesiastes*

Don't think there are no crocodiles because the water is calm.
MALAYAN PROVERB

Remember that there is nothing stable in human affairs; therefore avoid undue elation in prosperity, or undue depression in adversity.
SOCRATES

Too much taking heed is loss. GEORGE HERBERT

If one is forever cautious, can one remain a human being?
ALEXANDER SOLZHENITSYN

Avoiding danger is no safer in the long run than outright exposure. The fearful are caught as often as the bold. HELEN KELLER

The torment of precautions often exceeds the dangers to be avoided. It is sometimes better to abandon one's self to destiny.
NAPOLEON BONAPARTE

When a man feels the difficulty of doing, can he be other than cautious and slow in speaking? CONFUCIUS

Difficulties

Without the slightest doubt
Everyone's tormentor
Is the fact that to get out
Is harder than to enter.

Don't argue about the difficulties. The difficulties will argue for themselves. SIR WINSTON CHURCHILL

The only way round is through. ROBERT FROST

It is not the knowing that is difficult, but the doing. CONFUCIUS

To sow is less difficult than to reap.
JOHANN WOLFGANG von GOETHE

I sometimes suspect that half our difficulties are imaginary and that if we kept quiet about them they would disappear. ROBERT LYND

I prefer the sign NO ENTRANCE to the sign which says NO EXIT.
STANISLAW J. LEE

I have always liked things that are difficult, I have always had the urge to open forbidden doors, with a curiosity and an obstinacy that verge on masochism. JEANNE MOREAU

There are two ways of meeting difficulties: you alter the difficulties, or you alter yourself meeting them. PHYLLIS BOTTOME

Almost everything serious is difficult, and everything is serious.
RAINER MARIA RILKE

Bad is never good until worse happens. DANISH PROVERB

Never do a thing that you find difficult, because another person who finds it easy will beat you at the game. WILLIAM MORRIS

If you have had some hard bumps, you are probably traveling out of the rut. HERBERT V. PROCHNOW

Very often when one thinks of a way to get out of a difficulty, one gets into still greater difficulties. JEAN de la FONTAINE

If prolonged, it cannot be severe, and if severe, it cannot be prolonged.
LUCIUS ANNAEUS SENECA

They sicken of the calm that knows the storm. DOROTHY PARKER

Man is preceded by forest, followed by desert. GRAFFITO

Never trust the advice of a man in difficulties. AESOP

Settle one difficulty, and you keep a hundred others away.
CHINESE PROVERB

It is not always by plugging away at a difficulty and sticking at it that one overcomes it, but, rather, often by working on the one next to it. Certain people and certain things require to be approached on an angle.
ANDRE GIDE

Many things difficult to design prove easy to performance.
SAMUEL JOHNSON

A workable and effective way to meet and overcome difficulties is to take on someone else's problems. It is a strange fact, but you can often handle two difficulties—your own and somebody else's—better then you can handle your own alone. That truth is based on a subtle law of self-giving or outgoingness whereby you develop a self-strengthening in the process.
NORMAN VINCENT PEALE

A difficulty for every solution. LORD SAMUEL

The greater the difficulty, the greater the glory.
MARCUS TULLIUS CICERO

Many men owe the grandeur of their lives to their tremendous difficulties.
LAO-TSZE

No man ever sank under the burden of the day. It is when tomorrow's burden is added to the burden of today, that the weight is more than a man can bear.
GEORGE MACDONALD

There is nothing so easy that it becomes difficult when you do it with reluctance.
PUBLIUS TERENCE

Our strength often increases in proportion to the obstacles placed upon it. It is thus we enter upon the most perilous plans after having had the shame of failing in more simple ones.
RENE RAPIN

The greater the difficulty, the more glory in surmounting it. Skilful pilots gain their reputation from storms and tempests.
EPICURUS

Life affords no higher pleasure than that of surmounting difficulties, passing from one step of success to another, forming new wishes, and seeing them gratified.
SAMUEL JOHNSON

Problems

Most problems are always combined
And you never can beat the facts;
When something goes wrong, you are fined
But if it goes right, you are taxed.

Our problem is not what the dollar is worth at home or abroad—it's how to get hold of it whatever it's worth.
WILL ROGERS

You can only cure retail but you can prevent wholesale.
BROCK CHISHOLM

It is surprising how many improvements can come out of things that go wrong.
ANON

Although action is typical of the American style, thought and planning are not; it is considered heresy to state that some problems are not immediately or easily solvable.
DANIEL BELL

If I dealt in candles, the sun would never set.
YIDDISH PROVERB

Remove the cause and you remove the effect
LATIN PROVERB

It's a tough world for the American businessman. Every time he comes up with something new the Russians invent it a week later and the Japanese make it cheaper.
ANON

It is often wonderful how putting down on paper a clear statement of a case helps one to see, not perhaps the way out, but the way in.
ARTHUR CHRISTOPHER BENSON

The best way out is always through.
ROBERT FROST

He won't get to the root of his problem, because the root of his problem is himself.
CARROLL O'CONNOR

You often get a better hold upon a problem by going away from it for a time and dismissing it from your mind altogether.
DR. FRANK CRANE

There cannot be a crisis next week. My schedule is already full.
HENRY KISSINGER

In my experience, the worst thing you can do to an important problem is to discuss it.
SIMON GRAY

The chief cause of problems is solutions.
PAUL DICKSON

Problems are the price you pay for progress.
BRANCH RICKEY

Our major obligation is not to mistake slogans for solutions.
EDWARD R. MURROW

Better to go back than go wrong.
ANON

Have you got a problem? Do what you can where you are with what you've got. THEODORE ROOSEVELT

Nothing is particularly hard if you divide it into small jobs. HENRY FORD

One must avoid the urge to buy one's way out of problems by yielding to immediate pressures and ignoring the long run effects of the solution. PROFESSOR RAY E. BROWN

The trouble with show business is that the stars keep ninety per cent of my money. LORD GRADE

He who builds a better mousetrap these days runs into design difficulties, material shortages, patent-infringement suits, work stoppages, collusive bidding, discount discrimination—and taxes. H. E. MARTZ

A problem well stated is a problem half solved. CHARLES F. KETTERING

The world doesn't want to hear about the labor pains. It only wants to see the baby. JOHNNY SAIN

It looks like a flaw in the ointment. ANNIE LOTH

If you see ten troubles coming down the road, you can be sure that nine will run into the ditch before they reach you. CALVIN COOLIDGE

Where do you complain about the complaint department? LEOPOLD FECHTNER

I am more important than my problems. JOSE FERRER

A nuisance may be merely a right thing in the wrong place—like a pig in the parlor instead of the barnyard. JUSTICE GEORGE SUTHERLAND

Indecision and procrastination have never solved a single problem in the history of mankind, and they never will. HARRY A. BULLIS

A great man is one who seizes the vital issue in a complex question, what we might call the "jugular vein" of the whole organism—and spends his energies upon that. JOSEPH RICKABY

Money that is spent before it is earned usually buys nothing more than unhappiness. ANON

You never know where bottom is until you plumb for it.
FREDERICK LAING

I have yet to see any problem, however complicated, which, when you looked at it the right way, did not become still more complicated.
PAUL ANDERSON

Tragedy can be turned into comedy by sitting down.
DOROTHY L. SAYERS

Progress is the mother of problems. GILBERT KEITH CHESTERTON

The best way to escape from a problem is to solve it.
BRENDAN FRANCIS

When a problem presents itself, beware not to accept it at face value. A problem to others may be the means for you to become extremely wealthy. KURT HANKS

Learn to accept the inevitable in order to turn it into the useful.
CHARLES-MAURICE de TALLEYRAND

The field of consciousness is tiny. It accepts only one problem at a time. Get into a fist fight, put your mind on the strategy of the fight, and you will not feel the other fellow's punches.
ANTOINE de SAINT-EXUPERY

To get the kernel, you must crack the nut.
TITUS MACCIUS PLAUTUS

Approach each new problem not with a view of finding what you hope will be there, but to get the truth, the realities that must be grappled with. You may not like what you find. In that case you are entitled to try to change it. But do not deceive yourself as to what you do find to be the facts of the situation. BERNARD M. BARUCH

Basic problems do not fade away when unattended but thrive best when ignored and obscured. PROFESSOR RAY E. BROWN

Meet the first beginnings; look to the budding mischief before it has time to ripen to maturity. ANON

All the problems become smaller if you don't dodge them, but confront them. Touch a thistle timidly, and it pricks you; grasp it boldly, and its spines crumble. WILLIAM S. HALSEY

Let tears flow of their own accord: their flowing is not inconsistent with inward peace and harmony. SENECA

Fools

Never fools condemn
And never mistake it;
If it wasn't for them
We could not make it.

A fool and his money are soon parted. What I want to know is how they got together in the first place. CYRIL FLETCHER

There was a time when a fool and his money were soon parted, but now it happens to everybody. ADLAI STEVENSON

A fool and her money are soon courted. HELEN ROWLAND

In the postwar years, there were two born every minute.
P. J. O'ROURKE

April 1: This is the day upon which we are reminded of what we are on the other three hundred and sixty-four. MARK TWAIN

One of the wisest things my daddy ever told me was that "so-and-so is a damned smart man, but the fool's got no sense."
LYNDON BAINES JOHNSON

When he said we were trying to make a fool of him, I could only murmur that the Creator had beat us to it. GEORGE CHAPMAN

Of the whole rabble of thieves, the fools are the worst; for they rob you of both time and peace of mind. JOHANN WOLFGANG von GOETHE

Stupidity often saves a man from going mad.
OLIVER WENDELL HOLMES

If the fools do not control the world, it isn't because they are not in the majority.
EDGAR WATSON HOWE

The foolish and the dead alone never change their opinion.
JAMES RUSSELL LOWELL

In all companies there are more fools than wise men, and the greater part always get the better of the wiser.
FRANCOIS RABELAIS

If fifty men did all the work,
And gave the price to five,
And let those five make all the rules—
You'd say the fifty men were fools,
Unfit to be alive.
CHARLOTTE P. S. GILMAN

In any combat between a rogue and a fool the sympathy of mankind is always with the rogue.
HENRY LOUIS MENCKEN

A wise man who stands firm is a statesman, a foolish man who stands firm is a catastrophe.
ADLAI STEVENSON

A fool often fails because he thinks what is difficult is easy; a wise man, because he thinks what is easy is difficult.
JOHN CHURTON COLLINS

The fool knows after he's suffered.
HESIOD

None but a fool is always right.
AUGUST W. HARE

He that does not know a fool when he sees him is one himself.
BALTASAR BRACIAN

No man really becomes a fool until he stops asking questions.
CHARLES P. STEINMETZ

Luck sometimes visits a fool, but never sits down with him.
GERMAN PROVERB

If you are dealing with a fool, dictate, but never argue, for you will lose your labor and perhaps your temper.
OLIVER WENDELL HOLMES

A fool's paradise is a wise man's hell.
THOMAS FULLER

It is better to be born a beggar than a fool. SPANISH PROVERB

Wise people think all they say, fools say all they think. ANON

The best way to convince a fool that he is wrong is to let him have his own way. JOSH BILLINGS

The fool is not the man who merely does foolish things. The fool is the man who does not know enough to cash in on his foolishness.
ELBERT HUBBARD

To make a trade of laughing at a fool is the highway to become one.
THOMAS FULLER

A fool is his own informer. YIDDISH PROVERB

It is a stupidity second to none, to busy oneself with the correction of the world. JEAN BAPTISTE MOLIERE

Whoever catches the fool first is entitled to shear him.
EDGAR WATSON HOWE

A man may be as much a fool from the want of sensibility, as from the want of sense. ANNA JAMESON

Every man hath a fool in his sleeve. THOMAS FULLER

The treasure-house of a fool is in his speech, so that he can enrich himself by speaking ill of his betters TITUS MACCIUS PLAUTUS

Envy

One thought that takes a lot to chew
Is none the less a likely view;
That those to whom your envy's due
Are just as envious of you.

Too often it is the love of the other fellow's money which is the root of all evil. HERBERT V. PROCHNOW

Beggars do not envy millionaires, though of course they will envy other beggars who are more successful. BERTRAND RUSSELL

Envy has no holidays. FRANCIS BACON

Envy's a sharper spur than pay. JOHN GAY

Other people's eggs have two yolks. BULGARIAN PROVERB

The rich are more envied by those who have a little than by those who have nothing. CHARLES CALEB COLTON

Envy follows in the tracks of the wealthy. SOPHOCLES

What you can't have, abuse. ITALIAN PROVERB

We spend our time envying people whom we wouldn't wish to be.
JEAN ROSTAND

I think if you ask people what their concept of heaven is, they would say, if they are honest, that it is a big department store, with new things every week—all the money to buy them, and maybe a little more than the neighbor. ERICH FROMM

Though satisticians in our time have never kept the score,
Man wants a great deal here below and Woman even more.
JAMES THURBER

Nothing but a row of hooks to hang up grudges on. JOHN FOSTER

When I was young I thought Socialism was the mathematics of justice. Now I realize it is only the arithmetic of envy. MARTIN COLLINS

Riches rather enlarge than satisfy appetites. THOMAS FULLER

The dullard's envy of brilliant men is always assuaged by the suspicion that they will come to a bad end. MAX BEERBOHM

When envy, hate, fear are habitual, they are capable of starting genuine diseases DR. ALEXIS CARREL

It is better to envy wisdom than riches. GREEK PROVERB

Some folks rail against other folks, because other folks have what some folks would be glad of. HENRY FIELDING

Ah, but a man's reach should exceed his grasp. ROBERT BROWNING

I see nothing in the life of a rich man which the workman need envy, outside the regularity and security of his existence. ST. JOHN IRVINE

If your desires be endless, your cares and fears will be so too.
THOMAS FULLER

It is hard to endure envy, but much harder to have nothing worth envying. LATIN PROVERB

Envy is thin because it bites but never eats. SPANISH PROVERB

Riches have made more covetous men than covetousness hath made rich men. THOMAS FULLER

Envy and wrath shorten the life. *Ecclesiasticus*

Excess of wealth is cause of covetousness.
CHRISTOPHER MARLOWE

A man that is busy and inquisitive is commonly envious. For envy is a gadding passion, and walketh the streets, and doth not keep at home.
FRANCIS BACON

He is not poor that hath not much, but he that craves much.
THOMAS FULLER

People are crying up the rich and variegated plumage of the peacock; and he is himself blushing at the sight of his ugly feet.
ROBERT BROWNING

The envious man does not die only once but as many times as the person he envies lives to hear the voice of praise. BALTASAR GRACIAN

Greed

The amount that the needy
Would consider enough
Is refused by the greedy
Just like hogs in a trough.

The average prudent investor is a greedy son of a bitch. ANON

Much will have more. RALPH WALDO EMERSON

A poor man's roast and a rich man's death are sniffed far off. YIDDISH PROVERB

A money-grabber is anyone who grabs more than you can grab. ANON

The Chinese tell of a man who dreamed of gold, much gold, his heart's desire. He rose one day, and when the sun was high he dressed in his finest garments and went to the crowded market place. He stepped directly to the booth of a gold dealer, snatched a bag full of gold coins, and walked calmly away. The officials who arrested him were puzzled: "Why did you rob the gold dealer in broad daylight?" they asked. "And in the presence of so many people?" "I did not see any people," the man replied. "I saw only gold." LEWIS BINSTOCK

We want to clean out the pigsty, get rid of the pigs, and get out own snouts into the trough. ERNST ROHM

It makes no difference which side bread is buttered on . . . eat both sides. GERALD F. LIEBERMAN

No one bull-dog yet could eat
Any other bull-dog's meat;
If you have a good-sized bone,
Let the other dog alone. ANON

He is better with a rake than a fork. ENGLISH PROVERB

Though avarice will prevent a man from being necessitously poor, it generally makes him too timorous to be wealthy. THOMAS PAINE

To hazard much to get much has more of avarice than wisdom.
WILLIAM PENN

Greed's worst point is its ingratitude. LUCIUS ANNAEUS SENECA

Avarice walks among us disguised as ambition. EZRA J. MISHAN

Bit mouthfuls often choke. ITALIAN PROVERB

The natural man has only two primal passions—to get and beget.
SIR WILLIAM OSLER

We all risk being too greedy. JEAN de la FONTAINE

Avarice, the spur of industry. DAVID HUME

People who are greedy have extraordinary capacities for waste—they must take in too much. NORMAN MAILER

What kind of society isn't structured on greed? The problem of social organization is how to set up an arrangement under which greed will do the least harm; capitalism is that kind of a system.
MILTON FRIEDMAN

Suppose everybody cared enough, everybody shared enough? There is enough in the world for everyone's need, but not for everyone's greed.
FRANK BUCHMAN

Men would live exceedingly quiet if those two words, mine and thine, were taken away. ANAXAGORAS

If you would abolish avarice, you must abolish its mother, luxury.
MARCUS TULLIUS CICERO

A gross belly does not produce a refined mind. EDMUND FULLER

The greedy man is incontinent with a whole world set before him.
SA'DI

When all other sins are old, avarice is still young.
FRENCH PROVERB

Think not that a man will so much as lift up his little finger on your behalf, unless he sees his advantage in it. JEREMY BENTHAM

It is impossible to escape the impression that people commonly use false standards of measurement—that they seek power, success and wealth for themselves and admire them in others, and that they underestimate what is of true value in life. SIGMUND FREUD

Men hate the individual whom they call avaricious only because nothing can be gained from him. FRANCOIS VOLTAIRE

Greed lessens what is gathered. ARAB PROVERB

Avarice is more opposed to economy than liberality is.
FRANCOIS DUC de la ROCHEFOUCAULD

Avarice is as destitude of what is has, as poverty of what it has not.
PUBLILIUS SYRUS

Be charitable before wealth makes thee covetous.
SIR THOMAS BROWNE

Worry

All of your worries will go away
And ease your apprehension,
If you look at them another way
And call it nought but "tension."

The reason why worry kills more people than work is that more people worry than work. ROBERT FROST

When I look back on all these worries I remember the story of the old man who said on his deathbed that he had had a lot of trouble in his life, most of which had never happened. SIR WINSTON CHURCHILL

The happiest people are those who are too busy to worry in the daytime and too sleepy to worry at night. ANON

If there is a paradise, there are many natures who will always worry whether they ought not to be somewhere else. HENRY GREEN

People get so in the habit of worry that if you save them from drowning and put them on a bank to dry in the sun with hot chocolate and muffins, they wonder whether they are catching cold. JOHN JAY CHAPMAN

Worry, the interest paid by those who borrow trouble.
JUDGE GEORGE W. LYON

Worry is the interest paid on trouble before it falls due.
DEAN WILLIAM RALPH INGE

If you must worry, don't worry out loud. It wastes the time of others as well as your own. ARNOLD H. GLASGOW

Worry is impatience. AUSTIN O'MALLEY

Anxiety is fear of one's self. WILHELM STEKEL

Comedian Jerry Lewis was advised by his doctor. "Don't worry." Jerry countered, "How do you don't?" BOB HANSEN

You probably wouldn't worry about what people think of you if you could know how seldom they do! OLIN MILLER

Bacchus has drowned more men than Neptune.
GUISEPPE GARIBALDI

As a cure for worrying, work is better than whiskey.
THOMAS A. EDISON

But I'm not so think as you drunk I am. SIR JOHN SQUIRE

Never mind, dear, we're all made the same, though some more than others. NOEL COWARD

All moanday, tearsday, wailsday, thumpsday, frightday, shatterday.
JAMES JOYCE

The world is composed ot takers and givers. The takers may eat better, but the givers sleep better. BYRON FREDERICK

What my cup runneth over is me. ANON

It's no use crying over spilt milk: it only makes it salty for the cat.
ANON

It is a good thing that life is not as serious as it seems to a waiter.
DON HEROLD

Life is easier to take than you'd think: all that is necessary is to accept the impossible, do without the indispensable and bear the intolerable.
KATHLEEN NORRIS

It's no go my honey love, it's no go my poppet;
Work your hands from day to day, the winds will blow the profit.
The glass is falling hour by hour, the glass will fall for ever,
But if you break the bloody glass you won't hold up the weather.
LOUIS MACNEICE

If you're a hypochondriac, first class, you awaken each morning with the firm resolve not to worry; everything is going to turn out all wrong.
GOODMAN ACE

Worry affects circulation, the heart and the glands, the whole nervous system, and profoundly affects the heart. I have never known a man who died from overwork, but many who died from doubt.
DR. CHARLES MAYO

If I spent as much time doing the things I worry about getting done as I do worrying about doing them, I wouldn't have anything to worry about.
BERYL PFIZER

If you are standing upright, don't worry if your shadow is crooked.
CHINESE PROVERB

Steps a Person Can Take to Relieve Stress: Talk it out.
When something worries you, don't bottle it up. . . . Escape for a while. When things go wrong, it helps to escape from the painful problem for a while. . . . Work off your anger. Do something constructive with the pent-up energy. Pitch into some physical activity or work it out in tennis or a long walk. . . . Do something for others. If you feel yourself worrying about yourself all the time, try doing something for somebody else. . . . Take one thing at a time. Take a few of the most urgent tasks and pitch into them, one at a time, setting aside all the rest for the time being. Shun the "superman" urge. No one can be perfect in everything.
DR. NEIL SOLOMON

The growing American characteristically defends himself against anxiety by learning not to become too involved.
EDGAR ZODIAG FRIEDENBERG

Better be despised for too anxious apprehensions, than ruined by too confident security. EDMUND BURKE

The seven deadly sins . . . food, clothing, firing, rent, taxes, respectability, and children. GEORGE BERNARD SHAW

We live in an age of the overworked and the undereducated: the age in which people are so industrious that they become absolutely stupid. OSCAR WILDE

Anxiety is the price that must be paid for boundless opportunity, and not everyone can handle it. TED MORGAN

Worry is a form of fear and all forms of fear produce fatigue. A man who has learned not to feel fear will find the fatigue of daily life enormously diminished. BERTRAND RUSSELL

Waste not fresh tears over old griefs. EURIPIDES

I would rather worry without need than live without heed. PIERRE AUGUSTIN BEAUMARCHAIS

And as for me, let what will come, I can receive no damage from it, unless I think it a calamity; and it is in my power to think it none, if I so decide. MARCUS AURELIUS